2

Learn to Listen Listen to Learn

Academic Listening and Note-Taking

Third Edition

Roni S. Lebauer

Learn to Listen—Listen to Learn 2
Academic Listening and Note-Taking
Third Edition

Pearson Education, 10 Bank Street, White Plains, NY 10606

Staff credits: The people who made up the ***Learn to Listen—Listen to Learn 2, Third Edition*** team, representing editorial, production, design, and manufacturing are: Pietro Alongi, Rhea Banker, Dave Dickey, Jaime Lieber, Amy McCormick, Linda Moser, Carlos Rountree, Jennifer Stem, Paula Van Ells, and Dorothy Zemach.

Cover design: Barbara Sabella
Text design: Word & Image Design
Text composition: Word & Image Design
Text font: ITC Giovanni

Library of Congress Cataloging-in-Publication Data
Lebauer, R. Susan.
Learn to listen - listen to learn 2 : academic listening and note-taking / Roni S. Lebauer. — 3rd ed.
p. cm.
Includes bibliographical references and index.
ISBN-13: 978-0-13-814000-7 (pbk.)
ISBN-10: 0-13-814000-6 (pbk.)
1. Lecture method in teaching. 2. Listening. 3. Note-taking. 4. English language—Study and teaching—United States—Foreign speakers. I. Title.
LB2393.L43 2010
371.39'6--dc22
2009039949

ISBN-10: 0-13-814000-6
ISBN-13: 978-0-13-814000-7

Printed in the United States of America
8 9 10 –V057–15 14

CONTENTS

PREFACE

This book is designed to help advanced ESL/EFL students prepare for the demands of academic lecture comprehension and note-taking.

Listening to lectures and taking notes involves more than language skills alone. Rather, lecture comprehension and note-taking require skills in **evaluating information** (deciding what is important and needs to be noted), **organizing information** (seeing how ideas relate to each other), and **predicting information** (anticipating the content and direction of a lecture). This book teaches these skills and also includes exercises focusing on the acquisition of vocabulary and the **recognition of language cues** (lexical, grammatical, and paralinguistic cues) that are used in lectures to signal lecture organization.

One goal of this book is to **teach students *how* to listen to a lecture and take notes:** how to recognize lecture organization, use lecture cues and conventions that indicate organization and emphasis, recognize redundancy, and predict information. The text teaches these skills and provides numerous opportunities to practice them.

Another goal of this book is to **provide materials that replicate the style and function of academic lectures**. The lectures in the text have been selected to motivate students to listen, not just to complete a language task but also to gain knowledge about a variety of topics. These lectures cover a wide range of fields, and are accessible to the layperson yet still of interest to the specialist. The text also aims to simulate the lecture situation by allowing teachers to either deliver the lectures live (using the outlines in the Teacher's Manual), play recorded lectures given by a variety of speakers, or both. In addition, many activities in the book include excerpts from lectures originally given to audiences comprising native English speakers.

KEY CHANGES IN THE THIRD EDITION

- The overall organization of the book has been changed to allow teachers and students to proceed through the book more sequentially.
- Lectures have been updated and new lectures and excerpts have been added. Lecture topics continue to reflect a diversity of disciplines, including the arts, humanities, sciences, engineering, technology, and social sciences.
- Explanations have been simplified.
- Strategies for listening, note-taking, vocabulary aquisition, and studying are emphasized.
- "Replay Questions" activities have been added, drawing attention to specific idioms, facts, or attitudes.

- "Other Voices" follow-up exercises have been added to each lecture, giving exposure and practice to interaction typical in university settings (e.g., questions in class, office visits, small group discussions, informal banter among students after class). Not only do these exercises give students listening practice, but they also give insight into expectations and behavior on U.S. campuses.
- Post-lecture comprehension checks have been revised and, in addition to questions about facts from the lecture, also include inference and attitude questions. The range of formats for comprehension checks has been expanded beyond True/False, multiple-choice, short-answer, and essay questions to include graphic organizers and sequencing questions.
- Because many students are interested in taking the TOEFL® iBT test (which includes a lecture comprehension portion), question types typical of that test are also included throughout the text.
- Vocabulary practice has been expanded with each lecture unit containing at least three opportunities to learn and practice vocabulary and vocabulary development strategies. Academic Word List vocabulary has been highlighted and is practiced in multiple activities. Vocabulary is often recycled among lectures and activities so that repeated exposure in different settings can strengthen acquisition.
- Extension activities have been revised to include a range of activities exploring what students might "do" with academic content: research, presentations, and web browsing, along with general reading, writing, speaking, and listening activities, all provide additional opportunities to personalize and expand upon ideas raised in the lectures.

How to Use This Book

The text is divided into nine units. Units build upon previous units and recycle information learned. Throughout the book, strategies for college success—particularly for improving listening, note-taking, study skills habits, and vocabulary development—are highlighted.

- **Unit 1** is a pre-coursework evaluation, containing lectures and exercises that help the teacher evaluate students' levels prior to using this book (and help students self-evaluate and consider what they might need to concentrate on). The lecture in this section is related to academic listening, and thus it informs as well as tests.

- **Unit 2** aims to increase student awareness of lecture discourse, with lecture transcripts and exercises demonstrating the high degree of paraphrase and redundancy in lectures and the use of cues that introduce topics, signal organization, and conclude lectures. Through awareness and practice, students gain an understanding of how important these discourse factors are, enabling them to predict ideas and lecture direction. In Unit 2, students are examining lecture discourse by reading and discussing transcripts of authentic lectures.

- **Unit 3** allows students to hear authentic excerpts from lectures originally given in university or conference settings. The activities focus on predicting and confirming lecture direction from introductions and conclusions. In addition, students learn to recognize when lecturers go "off track" with digressions and when they get back "on track."

- **Unit 4** begins note-taking practice and instruction; it contains guidelines, information, and exercises on note-taking basics: noting key words, using symbols, and using space on the page to show relationships between ideas.

- **Unit 5** contains lectures and exercises on noting numbers, years, and statistics.

- **Units 6, 7, and 8**, "Listening for Organization, Parts 1, 2 and 3," introduce students to different organizational plans used in lectures. The students then practice comprehending, predicting, and taking notes from lecture excerpts that demonstrate these organizational plans. (As in Unit 3, excerpt material is truly authentic, coming directly from transcripts of college or conference lectures, originally given to English-fluent speaking audiences.)

- **Unit 9** is a consolidation unit, tying together and reviewing skills and strategies learned throughout the book. It contains two lectures that can serve as a final evaluation. Students are given less guidance and preparation for listening and note-taking, and they can use their notes as they might in a university situation. That is, they put them aside and use them as a reference in preparation for a quiz one or two weeks later.

PRE- AND POST-LECTURE ACTIVITIES

In Units 6 through 8, activities generally occur in the following sequence:

- **Discipline or Topic-Related Vocabulary.** Students can review words they already know and learn additional words in order to expand their vocabulary and general information schema for the topic covered in the lecture.

- **Pre-Lecture Discussion.** This activity provides background information, elicits interest, and provides a vehicle for the introduction of relevant vocabulary. The discussion often revolves around readings related to the topic.

- **Preparing for the Lecture.** Students discuss their expectations of the lecture based on the lecture title and the Pre-Lecture Discussion. This helps students build additional background knowledge. It also helps them make predictions about lecture content and organization before listening. Often, an introductory excerpt is played to give students continued practice in recognizing topic introductions.

- **Listening for the Larger Picture.** Students listen to the lecture once without taking notes and then answer questions. This helps them focus on getting the larger picture without becoming preoccupied with details. This section employs language similar to that used in the TOEFL® iBT listening sections, asking students to explain how the speaker accomplishes his or her goal (e.g., by listing, by comparing).

- **Organization.** Students read a summary of the lecture organization to affirm their initial comprehension or guide them toward better comprehension.

- **Defining Vocabulary.** Students listen to vocabulary from the lecture in different contexts and choose the correct meaning. Words marked with an asterisk are included in the AWL Vocabulary List.*

- **Listening and Note-Taking.** Students listen to the lecture a second time and take notes. Minimal comments in the margin guide the students by giving information about the lecture organization, while at the same time allowing them to develop their own note-taking style. After that, they revise or rewrite their notes so that they are better organized and include all relevant information.

- **"Replay" Questions.** Students listen to short excerpts from the larger lecture. These questions—often similar to those used in the listening section of the TOEFL® iBT exam—target vocabulary, content, inferences, lecturer's attitudes, lecturer's purpose for giving specific information, and lecturer's means of accomplishing a goal.

- **"Other Voices" Follow-Up.** After lectures, students listen to segments (often conversations) that relate to classroom concerns or that follow up on ideas presented in the lecture. Whereas lectures are largely unidirectional with the lecturer doing most or all of the talking, these listening activities typically focus on different types of interaction that take place in and around university lectures. This includes office visits (for multiple purposes such as career guidance, discussion of difficulties, inquiries about grades, sharing of information), end-of-class questions, and student-to-student discussions in and out of class. Questions in this section practice many skills tested in the listening section of the TOEFL® iBT exam and involve recognizing main topics, facts, speakers' purposes, attitudes, and methods.

---

* The Academic Word List was developed in 2000 by Averil Coxhead from a written academic corpus of material used in the fields of liberal arts, commerce, law, and science. It contains 570 words that appear most frequently in this corpus.

- **Post-Lecture Discussion.** Students participate in group discussions that encourage communication about issues raised in the lecture. Often these discussions involve additional related readings. This also serves to divert students' attention from the specific lecture details for a short while, forcing them to use their notes—rather than rely on memory—when doing the next activity.

- **Using Your Notes.** Students test the accuracy of their notes by using them to answer questions representative of those on university tests, such as True/False, multiple-choice, short-answer, and essay questions. In addition to recognition of stated information, students are asked to infer information and attitudes.

- **Comparing Ideas.** Students compare and discuss their notes to discover alternative and perhaps more effective ways to take notes.

- **Academic Word List Vocabulary.** These vocabulary exercises offer additional practice with academic vocabulary, derivations, and synonyms.

- **Using Vocabulary.** Students practice new vocabulary in different contexts, including conversational ones.

- **Retaining Vocabulary.** Using words employed in the lecture and activities, a specific vocabulary retention strategy is suggested and practiced.

- **Extension Activities.** Students use information from the lecture and related reading(s) in an extension Speaking and Listening Activity (such as a presentation or debate); a Writing Activity (such as an essay or letter); or a Reading/Research activity (such as Web site explorations and reports).

ANCILLARY MATERIALS

Audio CDs and a Teacher's Manual accompany this text.

- The **Audio CDs** provide exposure to a variety of speaking styles and can be a valuable resource for work in the classroom or language laboratory.

- The **Teacher's Manual** contains teaching suggestions, lecture outlines, lecture transcripts, exercise transcripts, and answer keys. It also has quizzes for the lectures in Unit 9.

Guidelines for Presenting Lectures

This book has been designed for maximum flexibility. Depending on the needs and expectations of their students, teachers have two options for presenting lectures. One option is to use the CDs, which allow teachers to expose students to a number of speaking styles and accents. Another option is for teachers to present live lectures to the class. To assist teachers in presenting lectures naturally, lecture outlines are included in the Teacher's Manual. The outlines give the basic information and structure of the lectures; it is up to the teacher to paraphrase, repeat, add information, go off on tangents, and summarize as necessary. The Teacher's Manual also includes transcripts of the recorded lectures to show how the lectures could sound when presented.

Live delivery of the lectures by ESL/EFL teachers cannot, of course, be completely authentic. Research has shown that ESL/EFL teachers adapt their language to fit the level of their nonnative speaker audiences. Although it may be impossible to completely erase all such "teacher talk" from lecture delivery, teachers should be aware of whether and how much they adapt their language. The goal should be to help students listen to lectures as they would be presented to native speaker listeners. Therefore, teachers should aim for their usual rate of speaking, vocabulary, and amount of repetition and paraphrase.

Notes on the "Authenticity" of Lectures

Lecture excerpts in Units 3, 6, 7, and 8 are truly authentic; that is, they were originally given by lecturers who were speaking to a native-English-proficient audience and who were unaware that their lectures would later be used for language teaching purposes. These lectures were transcribed verbatim and rerecorded professionally.

Longer lectures in this text have a different kind of authenticity. These lectures were delivered from outlines, not scripts, by native speakers to audiences composed of native and non-native English speakers. Lecturers were encouraged to speak naturally, but being aware that some in the audience were not fluent English speakers, they likely made some adaptations to their style. These lectures were recorded on site, transcribed, and later rerecorded professionally.

Together, these listening experiences expose students to material that is both accessible and authentic.

ACKNOWLEDGMENTS

Several people have helped me bring this book and its previous editions to its present form, and each of them deserves my sincere thanks:

- Miho Steinberg and Richard Day for first giving me release time from teaching duties in order to develop materials for an advanced ESL listening comprehension course;
- Ted Plaister and David Rickard for their encouragement of my work in listening comprehension and for providing technical resources and ideas that, way back then, provided stimuli for the first edition of this book;
- Ellen Broidy, Robert Ferguson, Michael Merrifield, Morgan Barrow, Larry Perez, Karah Street, Timothy Braatz, Tal Ben-Shahar, Jeremy Wolfe and the many other professors and speakers whose lectures and office visits I transcribed and used to examine lecture discourse and create many of the exercises in this book;
- Robin Scarcella and Vicki Bergman-Lanier for providing me with opportunities to pilot my original materials in their programs;
- The teachers who took extra time from their usually busy schedules to test this latest edition and previous versions and provide feedback: Aaron Albright, Martha Compton, Janice Jensen, Matthew Hunt, Lorraine Kumpf, Barbara Luthor, Wendy Maccoun, Kathy Smith, Susan Stern, Judy Tanka, Judy Via, and Angeliki Volksman;
- Colleagues and friends who provided creative and intellectual support: Jeanne Mazique, Jeffrey Clark, Michael Thorstensen, Jan Barber-Doyle, Laurel Connor;
- The editorial and production teams at Pearson Education for their enthusiasm, talent, and professionalism, along with Dorothy Zemach for her creativity, competence, and encouragement;
- The many anonymous reviewers and users whose thoughtful comments helped me revise and revise and revise;
- And finally, Michelle Rene-Ryan for being herself and being part of my life.

Roni S. Lebauer

CREDITS

Listening Selections and Text

Unit 2, Lecture Excerpts: Maslow's Hierarchy of Needs. Redrawn from Maslow AH: Motivation and Personality, Upper Saddle River, NJ, Prentice Hall; Robert Ferguson, Saddleback College, Psych 1: Intro to Psychology, Spring 2008; J. Greenberg, "Mental Health of Working Women," *Science News*, 117 (April 26, 1980), p. 266.

Unit 3, Lecture Excerpts: Helen Fisher, Rutgers U. "The Science of Love and the Future of Women" TED Talk 2/06; Tal Ben-Shahar, Harvard University, Positive Psychology: Psych 1504, Spring 2006; Michael D. Rugg, UCI, "Watching the brain at work: Imaging the formation and retrieval of memories," Irvine Health Foundation Lecture Series, 3/21/06; Robert Stickgold, Harvard Medical School "Memory and Dreams: What are they good for?" Irvine Health Foundation Lecture Series 3/16/04; Francesca Happe, King's College, London, "Autism: Cognitive Style Not Deficit?" Irvine Health Center Lectures, 1/25/06; Michael Merrifield, Saddleback College, Anthro 2, "Cultural Antropology" Spring 2008; Timothy Braatz, Saddleback College, History 22, "Basic U.S. History" Fall 2008; Ellen Broidy, lecture on "Topic Analysis," UC Irvine, 1988.

Unit 4, Lecture 2: J. Greenberg, "Mental Health of Working Women," *Science News*, 117 (April 26, 1980), p. 266.

Unit 5, Lecture 3: *American Heritage Dictionary Second College Edition*, Houghton Mifflin Company, Boston, MA, 1982; Sharon Begly with B.J. Sigesmund, "The Houses of Invention," *Newsweek* (Winter Extra 1997–1998), ©1997, Newsweek, Inc. All rights reserved. Reprinted by permission; *The Universal Almanac*, 1997, John W. Wright (Ed.), Andrews and McMeel, A Universal Press Syndicate Co., Kansas City, MO, 1996, pp. 591–593; Patrick Tucker, "Smart Fashion," The Futurist, Sept./Oct 2007, p. 68. **Unit 5, Lecture 4:** Emma Lazarus, "The New Colossus."

Unit 6, Lecture Excerpts: Tal Ben-Shahar, Harvard University, Positive Psychology: Psych 1504, Spring 2006; Jan Chipchase, "Our Cell Phones: Ourselves," TED Talk, March 2007; Steve Meier, University of Idaho, Psych 372; Ellen Broidy, Lecture on "Topic Analysis," UC Irvine, 1988. **Unit 6, Lecture 5:** Poem is one of many versions of Pastor Martin Niemoller's words that appeared in the *Congressional Record*, Oct. 14, 1968, p. 31636. **Unit 6, Lecture 6:** Morgan Barrows, office communication, Saddleback College, Fall 2008.

Unit 7, Lecture Excerpts: Karah Street, Saddleback College, Intro to Human Anatomy, Fall 2008; Michael Rost "On-line Summaries as Representations of Lecture Understanding" (1994), in John Flowerdew (Ed.) *Academic Listening: Research Perspectives*, Cambridge University Press, Cambridge, England: pp. 93–127; Tal Ben-Shahar, Harvard University, Positive Psychology: Psych 1504, Spring 2006; Steve Meier, University of Idaho, Psych 372; Helen Fisher, Rutgers U. "The Science of Love and the Future of Women" TED Talk 2/06; **Unit 7, Lecture 7:** Jane E. Stevens, "Cybersurgery," *Los Angeles Times* (December 4, 1995), p. B2. Reprinted by permission of the author; David R. Olmos, "Is There a Robot in the House?" *Los Angeles Times* (July 14, 1997), p. D1; Kathy A. Svitil, "Robotic Surgery," *Discover* (July 1998), p. 28. Copyright © 1998. Reprinted with permission of *Discover Magazine*; **Unit 7, Lecture 8:** Philip Yenawine, *How to Look at Modern Art*, Harry N. Abrams Inc. Pub., New York, 1991, pp. 143–144.

Unit 8, Lecture Excerpts: Tal Ben-Shahar, Harvard University, Positive Psychology: Psych 1504, Spring 2006; Ellen Broidy, Lecture on "Topic Analysis," UC Irvine, 1988; Jeremy Wolfe "The Battle of the Sexes: Love and Evolution" Intro to Psych, MIT ICW 900 Fall 04; Francesca Happe, King's College, London "Autism: Cognitive Style Not Deficit?" Irvine Health Center Lectures, 1/25/06; Marc D. Hauser, Harvard University: Wild Minds: What Animals Really Think"; Irvine Health Foundation Lecture Series, 3/27/01; James McGaugh, Director, Center for the Neurobiology of Learning and Memory and Research, Professor, Department of Neurobiology and Behavior, UC Irvine "The Magic of Memory: Peeking Behind the Brain's Curtain," Irvine Health Foundation Lecture Series May 22, 2002; **Unit 8, Lecture 9:** Elizabeth Hall, "How Cultures Collide," *Psychology Today* (July 1976), pp. 66–74; Kurien Joseph, "Cultural Differences in International Business," *Export Import Trade Flash* (Oct. 1–15, 1997). Reprinted with permission of Sunil Sudhakar; **Unit 8, Lecture 10:** "I Didn't Know That," *L.A. Times*, 7/31/97. Frederick K. Lutgens and Edward J. Tarbuck, *Foundations of Earth Science*, Prentice Hall, Upper Saddle River, NJ, 1996; Frederick K. Lutgens and Edward J. Tarbuck, *Essentials of Geology, 6e*, Prentice Hall, Upper Saddle River, NJ, 1998, p. 292. Reprinted by permission of Prentice Hall; Richard C. Paddock and Robert Lee Hotz, "Warning from Space?" *Los Angeles Times* (April 9, 1998), p. B2. Copyright ©1998 *Los Angeles Times*. Reprinted by permission; Terry R. West, *Geology Applied to Engineering*, Prentice Hall, NJ, 1994.

Unit 9, Lecture 11: "Perfectionism," University of Illinois at Urbana-Champaign Counseling Center Publication; David Burns, "The Perfectionist's Script for Self-defeat," Psychology Today (November 1980), pp. 34–52. Reprinted with permission from Psychology Today Magazine. Copyright © 1980 Sussex Publishers, Inc.; **Unit 9, Lecture 12:** Marshall, Elizabeth L. 1999. *High-Tech Harvest: A Look at Genetically Engineered Foods*, Franklin Watts, Grolier Publishing, NY and http/www.ecohealth101.org/whats_left/eat6.html; Union of Concerned Scientists Web site: http://www.ucsusa.org/food_and_environment/genetic_engineering/what-is-genetic-engineering.html; http://www.pollingreport.com/science.htm (reporting on genetic engineering polls done by CBS News/New York Times Poll, April 25-29, 2008; Gallup Poll, July 7-10, 2005; ABC News Poll, July 9-13, 2003; ABC News.com Poll, June 13-17, 2001; Pew Initiative on Food and Biotechnology Poll conducted by the Mellman Group and Public Opinion Strategies, Jan. 22-28, 2001; The Harris Poll, June 8-12, 2000).

Photos

Pages 84, 113, Associated Press. **Page 163**, © Shutterstock. **Page 120**, Copyright © Harry Callahan. Courtesy of the National Gallery of Art. **Page 121** (tl), Franz Kline, *Painting Number 2*, 1954. Oil on canvas, 6′ 8″ x 8′ 9″ (204.3 x 271.6 cm). The Museum of Modern Art, New York. Mr. and Mrs. Joseph H. Hazen and Mr. and Mrs. Francis F. Rosenbaum Funds. Photograph © 1999 The Museum of Modern Art, New York; (tr), Edgar Degas, *The Orchestra of the Opera*. c. 1870. Musee d'Orsay, Paris, France. Photo by Erich Lessing/Art Resource; (cl), The Metropolitan Museum of Art. All rights reserved; (cr), Copyright the Dorothea Lange Collection, The Oakland Museum of California, City of Oakland. Gift of Paul S. Taylor; (b) Photograph Copyright © 1999. Whitney Museum of American Art.

Illustrations

Pages 1, 9, 31, 43, 61, 70, 83, 95, 130, 131, 143, 171, Dusan Petricic. **Pages 2, 11, 13, 15, 23, 41, 51, 53, 105, 157, 172, 180**, Andy Myer. **Page 70** (a), Copyright © ARS/SPADEM 1987; (b, c), reprinted with permission of Amnesty International, International Secretariat, 1 Easton Street, London WC1X 8DJ, United Kingdom.

STARTING OUT: PRE-COURSEWORK EVALUATION

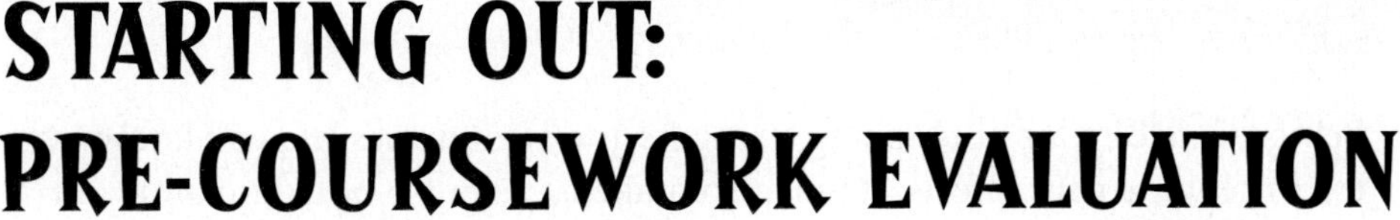

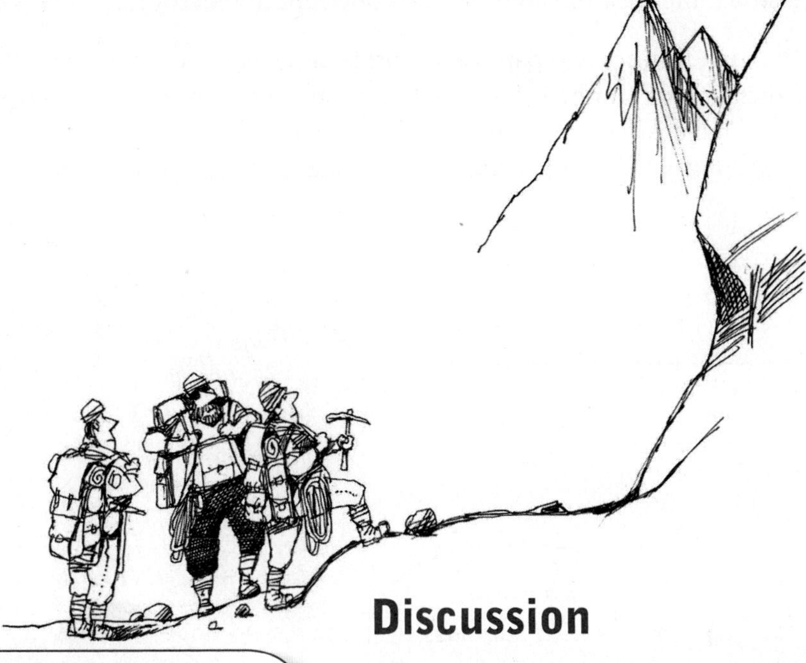

Goals

- Evaluate listening comprehension skills
- Evaluate note-taking skills
- Evaluate ability to note numbers

Discussion

Listening to Lectures

1. Rank the following from easiest (1) to hardest (5) for you:
   ____ listening to informal conversations outside of class
   ____ listening to in-class discussions
   ____ listening to "audio" media (e.g., radio podcasts)
   ____ listening to lectures with no teacher-student interaction
   ____ listening to lectures with some teacher-student interaction

   Explain your rankings.

2. What specific challenges do you face when you listen to a lecture in English?

3. Do you face the same challenges when you listen to a lecture in your native language?

4. Do you usually take notes when you listen to lectures in your native language? How well do you take notes in your native language? How does this compare to listening to lectures in English and taking notes?

Evaluating Listening Comprehension and Note-Taking Skills

Being aware of your note-taking strengths and weaknesses lets you know where to concentrate your efforts. It will also make it easier for both you and your instructor to measure your progress throughout this course.

This unit features two parts of a short lecture about academic listening and then a dictation of numbers. You will take notes and then use them to complete a chart and answer questions. After the activities, both you and your teacher will evaluate your listening comprehension and note-taking abilities.

LECTURE 1

Academic Listening (Linguistics)

ACTIVITY 1 LISTENING AND NOTE-TAKING (PART 1)

The first part of this linguistics lecture focuses on the differences between listening to lectures and listening in everyday situations. Listen and take notes on a separate piece of paper. Then use your notes to complete the chart.

	LECTURE	EVERYDAY LISTENING SITUATION
Language		
Interaction		
Expectations		

Self-Evaluation

1. How would you describe your ability to comprehend this lecture?

   ___ Excellent ___ Very Good ___ Good ___ Fair ___ Poor

2. How would you describe your ability to take notes while listening to this lecture?

   ___ Excellent ___ Very Good ___ Good ___ Fair ___ Poor

ACTIVITY 2 LISTENING AND NOTE-TAKING (PART 2)

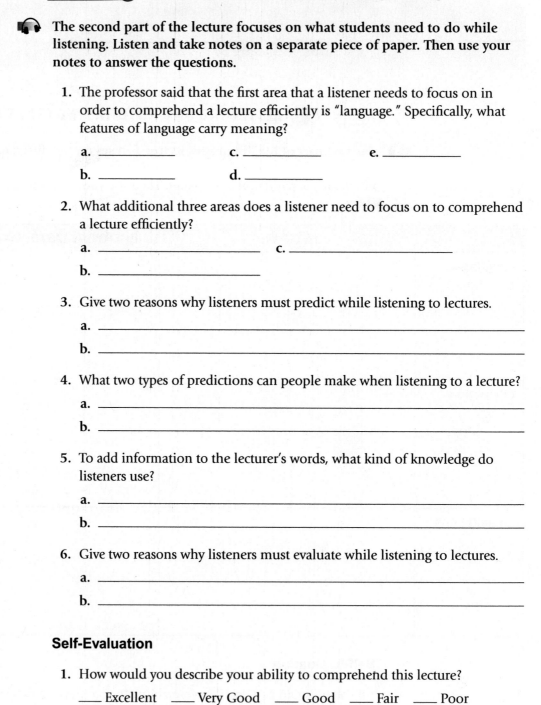

The second part of the lecture focuses on what students need to do while listening. Listen and take notes on a separate piece of paper. Then use your notes to answer the questions.

1. The professor said that the first area that a listener needs to focus on in order to comprehend a lecture efficiently is "language." Specifically, what features of language carry meaning?

   a. ____________ **c.** ____________ **e.** ____________

   b. ____________ **d.** ____________

2. What additional three areas does a listener need to focus on to comprehend a lecture efficiently?

   a. ________________________ **c.** ________________________

   b. ________________________

3. Give two reasons why listeners must predict while listening to lectures.

   a. ____

   b. ____

4. What two types of predictions can people make when listening to a lecture?

   a. ____

   b. ____

5. To add information to the lecturer's words, what kind of knowledge do listeners use?

   a. ____

   b. ____

6. Give two reasons why listeners must evaluate while listening to lectures.

   a. ____

   b. ____

Self-Evaluation

1. How would you describe your ability to comprehend this lecture?

   ___ Excellent ___ Very Good ___ Good ___ Fair ___ Poor

2. How would you describe your ability to take notes while listening to this lecture?

   ___ Excellent ___ Very Good ___ Good ___ Fair ___ Poor

ACTIVITY 3 POST-LECTURE DISCUSSION

Discuss the following questions in small groups.

1. According to the lecture, why might nonnative speakers of English have a hard time listening to lectures and taking notes?

2. What do you need to change or improve to be a better listener and note-taker?

ACTIVITY 4 DICTATION OF NUMBERS: AN EVALUATION

Listen to statements containing numbers. Write the numbers that you hear.

1. Anton Chekhov was born in _____________ and died in _____________.

2. Kites were known in China as early as _____________. The first reference to kites in Europe was found in _____________.

3. Mount Kilimanjaro is _____________ meters high.

4. The Sahara Desert is _____________ square miles.

5. Mercury's distance from the sun is _____________ miles.

6. Pluto's distance from the sun is _____________ miles.

7. In 2007, the percentage of the population under 15 was _____________ in Germany, _____________ in the United States, and _____________ in Ethiopia.

8. In a 2005 study of computer use, _____________ Canadians and _____________ of Americans sat in front of computer screens at least occasionally.

9. A major earthquake occurred in Iran on _____________. This earthquake measured _____________ on the Richter scale and caused more than _____________ deaths and _____________ injuries.

10. The board measured _____________ feet in length, _____________ inches in width, and _____________ inch in depth.

Self-Evaluation

1. How would you describe your ability to comprehend the numbers?

   ___ Excellent ___ Very Good ___ Good ___ Fair ___ Poor

2. What kind of numbers were hardest for you? Dates? The *-teen* versus *-ty* endings such as *18* and *80*? Large numbers? Fractions (such as $\frac{1}{5}$)? Percentages (*45%*)? Ratios (*1 in 10*)? Decimals (*3.7*)?

Teacher's Note-Taking Feedback Form

Your teacher will use a form similar to the one below when commenting on your notes in this class.

Note-Taking Feedback Form

Name ____________________

Date ____________ Lecture ____________

ORGANIZATION OF IDEAS[1]

___ You organize while you take notes. Good.

___ Your notes visually represent the relationship between ideas. Good.

___ Your notes reflect some attempt at visually representing the relationship between ideas, but could use more work.

___ Your notes are a little unclear; it's not always possible to see the relationship between ideas. Organize your notes to emphasize main ideas and show the relationships between ideas. Use visual cues such as indenting or drawing lines to show how pieces of information relate to other pieces of information. Use headings to label sections and show how ideas are related.

___ Your notes seem random. Evaluate as you listen to get the main points first. Add details when you have time or when you rewrite your notes.

___ You're writing down too much, including unimportant words and information. Note the minimum number of key words necessary for noting important information. This will allow you more time while listening to understand and evaluate ideas.

Additional comments about organization:

____

____

____

ACCURACY AND COMPLETENESS OF NOTES

___ You correctly noted most points, both major and minor ones. Good.

___ You noted most points (especially the major ones) but missed or misunderstood (a few/many) minor ones. It's good that you are able to discriminate between major ideas and minor ones. Practice and increased fluency in English will help you note more details.

___ You missed or misinterpreted (a few/many) major ideas and (a few/many) minor ideas. Get the major points first. If you have more time, note details related to these major points.

[1] Unit 4 introduces the ideas of noting key words and organizing notes while listening.

____ You may be noting too few key words. Without more key words, your notes will not be helpful later. Revise or rewrite your notes as soon as possible after lectures so that you can add information that you remember or talk to another student or the instructor after the lecture about what you missed.

Additional comments about accuracy and completeness of notes:

____

____

____

ACCURACY OF NOTING NUMBERS[2]

_____ You noted most numbers correctly. Good.

_____ You missed or misinterpreted a few numbers.

_____ You missed or misinterpreted many numbers.

Additional comments about accuracy of noting numbers:

____

____

____

OVERALL EVALUATION

____

____

____

____

____

____

____

____

____

____

[2] Unit 5, in particular, focuses on noting numbers.

Student's Goal-Setting Form

Complete the following chart with information about your current study habits and situation and your listening and note-taking goals. Make your goals realistic, specific, and measurable. For example, instead of saying "I'm going to improve my listening," say, "I'm going to record the news in English every day and watch it twice" or "I'm going to create flashcards to practice 25 new vocabulary words every week."

Refer to your goals regularly throughout this course to make sure you are meeting them.

Name: ______________________ Date: ____________

Major field of study: ______________________

Courses I'm taking now where I'll be listening to English: ______________________

____

Courses I'll probably be taking in the future where I'll be listening to English: ______________________

____

Places where I listen to English now outside of class: ______________________

____

Hours I spend listening to English • in class ________ • out of class ________

Ways I could practice listening to English more: ______________________

____

____

____

My challenges when listening to English: ______________________

____

____

____

Ideas on how I can overcome these challenges: ______________________

____

____

____

My listening and note-taking goals for this semester: ______________________

____

____

____

THE STRUCTURE OF A LECTURE

Goals

- Increase awareness of lecture design
- Increase ability to predict information, including content and organizational direction in lectures

Discussion

Psychology and Language

1. What kinds of things are studied in psychology classes?
2. Have you ever taken a psychology class? What did you like or dislike about it? What kinds of things did you study?
3. Do you think there are some personality traits that make it easier for some people to learn languages? What personality traits do you have that make it easier or harder for you to learn foreign languages?
4. What are some differences between reading and listening for information? Which do you prefer, and why?

Comparing the Language of Lecturing to the Language of Writing

Imagine you're reading in a psychology textbook about one theory of human psychological development: Abraham Maslow's "hierarchy of needs." You read this paragraph and see the chart below.

> Abraham Maslow, along with other humanists, stated that the goal of every individual is to reach his or her maximal potential; that is, "self-actualization." However, before people can reach the self-actualization stage, they must go through other stages. First, they have to meet physiological and basic survival needs (air, water, food). Next…

Now imagine that you were listening to a lecturer *telling* you exactly the same information. Here are the words that a professor used in his Introduction to Psychology class:

Okay, let's move on with Maslow … now if you haven't heard of Maslow's hierarchy of needs you've been living on the moon. … In Maslow … we're going to talk about some ages and stages … everybody has an individual maximum potential … and the goal of every individual is to reach that individual maximum potential. That's Maslow, Rodgers, some of these infamous humanists … you know everybody's got an individual maximum potential and the goal is to reach that individual maximum potential … by the way which is self-actualization … your individual maximum potential is self-actualization … which means … that's it … that's your individual maximum potential … self actualization … that's it … we're always trying to achieve it … but … before you can work on self-actualization you have to go through these other stages first … you can't just go out and get self-actualized … and I'm going to … this is where I'm going to make it come alive and give you some examples here … first of all you have to go through the physical stage … this would be like the caveman/cavewoman days … physical … I mean this is like survival … you've got to have enough air to breathe … you've got to have enough water to drink … and you've got to have enough food to eat … and if you don't have that you can't be self actualized … according to Maslow … I mean it's pretty obvious here … you're struggling around as a caveman/cavewoman … and you're running around there trying to get the fish and the saber-toothed tiger is after you … and you know it's … you're stuck there … you're stuck there.… You're stuck in that physical thing … you're not even trying to … be the best you can be … you're stuck in that physical thing, trying to survive … According to Maslow the next stage would be …

Self Actualization
Esteem Needs
Self-esteem
Recognition
Status
Social Needs
Sense of Belonging
Love
Safety Needs
Security
Protection
Physiological Needs
Hunger
Thirst

The information in the textbook and the lecture is essentially the same, but as you can see, it is presented very differently.

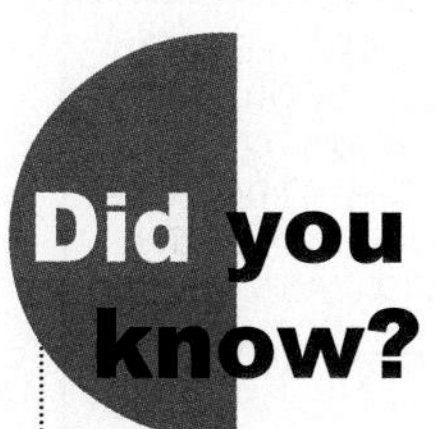

Before Maslow's work, most psychology had been concerned with the abnormal and the ill. Maslow focused on positive mental health.

Exercise 1

Compare the textbook paragraph and the lecture excerpt. Explain the ways in which the two presentations differ.

TEXTBOOK PARAGRAPH	LECTURE EXCERPT

B Noticing Lecture Structure and Cues

CUES TO TOPIC INTRODUCTIONS

In the lecture excerpt, you probably noticed explicit directions (cues) to guide your listening. One of these is the *cue to a topic introduction.*

Example

cues to topic introduction

(Okay,) (let's move on) with Maslow …

Written texts don't need these cues to topic introductions for a couple of reasons. First, written text is fixed, so a reader can return and reread if necessary. Second, the paragraphs in written text generally focus on one main idea contained in a topic sentence, with new ideas indicated by new paragraphs.

A speaker, on the other hand, uses both verbal and nonverbal cues to indicate the beginning of a new idea. The speaker may pause longer between the end of one section and the beginning of another, or the speaker may use a specific language cue to mark a new idea.

LISTENING AND NOTE-TAKING STRATEGY

Listen for cues to topic introductions. Some are specific, such as "Let's look at X," "Today we're going to talk about X," or "Let's move on to X." Others may not be as specific ("All right," "Now"), but they can still give you a hint that the speaker is starting a new idea.

You will learn more about these cues in Unit 3.

CUES TO ORGANIZATION

Both writers and lecturers organize their ideas to present them clearly with phrases such as "the first example," "the second point," "on the other hand," and so on. These cues help you predict the lecture's organization and also help you plan your note-taking (e.g., by starting a numbered list after you hear "the first reason").

Example

cues to organization

before you can work on self-actualization you have to go through these other stages first … you can't just go out and get self-actualized … and I'm going to … this is where I'm going to make it come alive and give you some examples here … first of all you have to go through the physical stage …

What do you expect the lecturer to do next in this lecture?

LISTENING AND NOTE-TAKING STRATEGY

Listen for cues to organization that will help you predict what the lecturer will say. This will help you organize your notes and decide what is important to note.

In Units 6, 7, and 8, you will learn more about specific cues to organization.

CUES TO TOPIC CONCLUSIONS

The same psychology professor wanted to talk about other models of psychological development. He finished with one model and then moved on to another like this:

Example

cue to topic conclusion — cue to topic introduction

… (and so) Piaget is basically a childhood model … and (let's move on to) the next one here and talk about Kohlberg … you're going to get so sick of ages and stages today …

Notice that when the lecturer finished describing Piaget's model, he attempted to tie the preceding ideas together by saying "and so" and summarizing the preceding ideas with a conclusion. After that, he used the cue to topic introduction "let's move on to" to show that he was ready to go to a new idea.

LISTENING AND NOTE-TAKING STRATEGY

Listen for cues telling you that the speaker is finishing an idea. Listen for a conclusion or a summary. If the lecture is not over, get ready for a new topic introduction.

You will learn more about cues to conclusions in Unit 3.

Understanding the Role of Paraphrase, Repetition, Exemplification, and Digression

Written language uses much less repetition and paraphrase than spoken language. Writers need to state an idea only once because readers can reread an idea as many times as necessary. However, lecturers need to give listeners time to think about or take notes on what they have heard. Lecturers do this by

- Paraphrasing (i.e., restating ideas using different words)
- Repetition
- Exemplification (i.e., giving examples and further details)

Paraphrase, repetition, and exemplification give the listener time to better understand the speaker's ideas, rather than introducing new information. They emphasize the importance of a particular idea or concept. Paraphrases and repetitions do not need to be noted a second time unless you missed the information the first time. Examples can be useful to note, however, because they explain ideas. Furthermore, some instructors will ask for examples on quizzes and exams.

Lecturers also digress more often than writers do. A story or connected idea might come to them as they are speaking, or they may judge from audience feedback that it would be appropriate to include a joke or a story. Writers can edit their digressions when they realize they are off topic; lecturers cannot. Use the time during digressions to just listen and take a break from note-taking, but be alert for cues that indicate the lecturer is returning to the scheduled topic.

Exercise 2

Reexamine the lecture excerpt about Maslow's theory. Work with a partner and label each of the circled expressions as a repetition, paraphrase, example, or digression.

Okay, let's move on with Maslow … now if you haven't heard of Maslow's hierarchy of needs you've been living on the moon … (laughter) … hopefully I can give you a little more insight into it … I know … I took an automobile mechanics class on this campus … learn how to work on a car … and he had Maslow's hierarchy of needs in there … (laughter) and I … you … you've got to be self-actualized if you're going to be working on a transmission… Okay … in Maslow … we're going to talk about some ages and stages … everybody has an individual maximum potential … and the goal of every individual is to reach that individual maximum potential. That's Maslow, Rodgers, some of these infamous humanists … you know everybody's got an individual maximum potential and the goal is to reach that individual maximum potential …

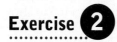

digression

Repetition

Ex.

Exampl.

by the way which is self-actualization … your individual maximum potential is self-actualization … which means … that's it … that's your individual maximum potential … self actualization … that's it … we're always trying to achieve it … but … before you can work on self-actualization you have to go through these other stages first … you can't just go out and get self-actualized … and I'm going to … this is where I'm going to make it come alive and give you some examples here … first of all you have to go through the physical stage … this would be like the caveman/cavewoman days … physical … I mean this is like survival … you've got to have enough air to breathe … you've got to have enough water to drink … and you've got to have enough food to eat … and if you don't have that you can't be self actualized … according to Maslow … I mean it's pretty obvious here … you're struggling around as a caveman/cavewoman … and you're running around there trying to get the fish and the saber-toothed tiger is after you … and you know it's … you're stuck there … you're stuck there…. You're stuck in that physical thing … you're not even trying to … be the best you can be … you're stuck in that physical thing, trying to survive … according to Maslow the next stage would be …

LISTENING AND NOTE-TAKING STRATEGY

Lecturers spend time paraphrasing, repeating, exemplifying, and digressing. Use this time to decide what is important and what to note.

THERE ARE REPORTS OF A CONFLAGRATION … WHAT I MEAN TO SAY IS … UH … THAT IS… BY "CONFLAGRATION" I WANT TO INDICATE… FIRE!!

Key Differences between the Language of Lecturing and the Language of Writing

Exercise 3

The purpose of this exercise is to identify cues and extra information in a lecture excerpt. This can help you understand the overall organization and recognize the main ideas. The excerpt includes the remainder of the lecture on Maslow's theory.

Directions

1. Listen to and read both of the excerpt sections (below and on the next page). Try to get a sense of what the lecturer is saying. (First refer back to the diagram on page 10.)
2. In the first section, notice that all of the cues have been circled. Notice that all of the repetitions, paraphrases, examples, and digressions have been crossed out.
3. Do the same in the second section: Circle all the cues and cross out all of the repetitions, paraphrases, examples, and digressions.
4. Compare and discuss your choices with a classmate. Your answers don't have to be exactly the same, but you should be able to justify your decisions.

cues to topic introduction

 *Okay, let's move on with Maslow … ~~now if you haven't heard of Maslow's hierarchy of needs you've been living on the moon … hopefully I can give you a little more insight into it … I know … I took an automobile mechanics class on this campus … learn how to work on a car … and he had Maslow's hierarchy of needs in there … (laughter) and I … you … you've got to be self-actualized if you're going to be working on a transmission.~~… Okay … in Maslow … we're going to talk about some ages and stages … everybody has an individual maximum potential … and the goal of every individual is to reach that individual maximum potential. That's Maslow, Rodgers, some of these infamous humanists … ~~you know everybody's got an individual maximum potential and the goal is to reach that individual maximum potential~~ … by the way which is self-actualization … ~~your individual maximum potential is self-actualization … which means … that's it … that's your individual maximum potential … self actualization … that's it … we're always trying to achieve it … but~~… before you can work on self-actualization you have to go through these other stages first … ~~you can't just go out and get self-actualized~~ … and I'm going to …*

cues to topic organization

this is where I'm going to make it come alive and give you some examples here … first of all you have to go through the physical stage … ~~*this would be like the caveman/cavewoman days … physical … I mean this is like survival … you've got to have enough air to breathe … you've got to have enough water to drink … and you've got to have enough food to eat … and if you don't have that you can't be self actualized … according to Maslow… I mean it's pretty obvious here … you're struggling around as a caveman/cavewoman … and you're running around there trying to get the fish and the saber-toothed tiger is after you … and you know it's … you're stuck there … you're stuck there.… You're stuck in that physical thing … you're not even trying to … be the best you can be … you're stuck in that physical thing, trying to survive*~~ … according to Maslow *the next stage would be* …

after physical then the safety thing shows up … you have to be able to live … I mean … if somebody is after you there and somebody is going to kill you … or you're in a high-stress occupation or in a high-unsafe occupation then you might be stuck in that second one there … but again we're going back to the caveman/cavewoman who are running around there with the saber-toothed tiger trying to get them … and uh … safety! … and other people trying to kill them! … well, I don't imagine that any of you are stuck there.… How many of you are in a gang? Don't raise your hand back there … (laughter) *no, he didn't raise his hand … if you're in a gang maybe they're shooting at you every day … if you're a cop or a firefighter maybe that's the deal … maybe that's your safety issue … not many of you are stuck there … well, how about "love"? … Okay so that's a little higher, right? … so relationship? Significant other? Permanent partner? Family? Support system? Maybe some of you are kind of stuck there … maybe you don't have that taken care of … nailed down … yet … so ... you know … what Maslow is saying … you really can't move on to self-actualization … we'll talk about that in a minute ... until you've gone through these other things … well this is really, really important to have a support system … and then "self-esteem" … "self-esteem" meaning that people … you feel good about yourself … people … people … you're in demand … maybe ... people … you feel really good about yourself … people look toward … people look up to you … people ask you for … for things … people believe you can … they believe you're sort of.… There's a lot of aspects of self-esteem but you basically feel good about yourself … um … and then self-actualization … Okay let's talk about self-actualization …*

Using Context and Prediction to Get Main Ideas

Listeners might miss information for a number of reasons (e.g., inadequate vocabulary, daydreaming, outside noise); however, they don't need to catch every word to understand main ideas. Listeners use cues to predict the lecture's direction, and also to fill in missed words and ideas. They also use their own experiences, logic, and knowledge of the subject matter to guess information they missed.

Exercise 

The following excerpt is a later part of the lecture about Jean Piaget's theory of child development. Many words and ideas have been omitted. In some cases, you can guess what has been left out; in other cases, you may not be sure.

Directions

1. Listen to and read the entire excerpt. Do not spend time trying to figure out the missing word(s); just try to get the main ideas.
2. Fill in the chart that follows the lecture based on the information you heard and read.
3. Compare your answers with a classmate.

What we are going to talk about here are the stages of Piaget … first they're going to be sensor-motor … the sensor-motor stage is birth to two years … the first two years of life Piaget would call "sensor-motor" … so we're not talking about … we already talked about language … we already talked about motor skills … we're not going to talk about that again … but we are going to talk about objects … objects … meaning people out there … things out there … Piaget says you know what? … the first couple of weeks after the baby comes home … I mean what's the first thing you all got? ... what's the first thing that someone bought you when you were a baby? … it was a mobile … it was one of those things that you hang on the crib … you screw it on the crib … it hangs over the crib and let's say there are butterflies flying around on little things … little plastic butterflies … that's the first thing you had … everybody has one ... or had one … so kids back from the hospital, kids just about a week old, two weeks old ... all of these big faces are looking at the kid in this ... in this ... laying there you know … and these butterflies are flying around there and everyone's going "oh look, look, isn't he cute! Here's mommy and here's daddy … here's the mobile and here are the butterflies" … Piaget would say kind of like you know what? … just save your breath on this one … because the child is struggling with object recognition here … object recognition … in other words,

… well … after recognition, after a couple of weeks … or a month or so … the child

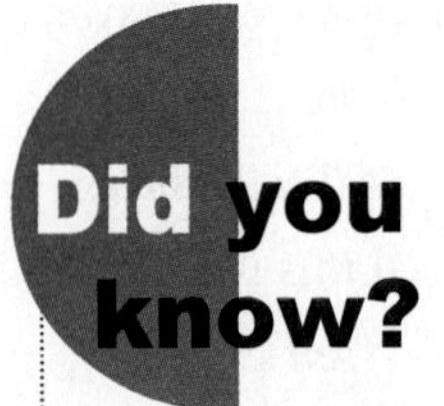

Infants as young as 2 weeks of age have color vision and can distinguish a red object from a green one.

recognizes the parents and the child recognizes that "hey there's other things out there ... people are looking at me once in a while and there's this thing hanging over the crib with the butterflies" ... then they're going to struggle with control *... they're going to get a little more sophisticated here ... so* recognition *is ... will go on for the first couple of weeks ... they'll struggle with that ... and it's basically* instinct *here ...* recognition *is instinct ... I mean the kid feels a hunger pain and cries "Oh" ... somebody ... it's just* instinct *... there's no control here ... they're not ... they're not doing it on purpose ...* but *after about a month or so ... which is going to be different ... not only now do they but* now whether they get a hunger pang or not *...* control *issues ... and it's the same with the mobile ... I mean this thing hanging over there with the butterflies ... they uh ... the parents walk by and the weight of their bodies stirring up some air and the butterflies move and the kid sees this ... but the kid didn't do anything about it ... the kid didn't do it on purpose ... but a couple weeks later,*

you know ... see ... we're getting more and more sophisticated here ... okay ... permanency *... this is very abstract okay ... and Piaget will say that this permanency switch doesn't really get thrown until about 8 months ... so if you've got an 8-month-old kid here ... um ... um ... you know they've got recognition and they've got control but they haven't got the permanency thing until after about 8 months ... so ... uh ... let's talk about it here ...*

Fill in the chart about the "sensor-motor" stage of development, according to Piaget.

	CHARACTERISTIC DEVELOPMENT AT THIS STAGE (WHAT CAN THEY DO? WHAT ARE THEY STILL STRUGGLING WITH?)	EXAMPLES
Younger than 2 weeks		
6 weeks old		
8 months old		

LISTENING AND NOTE-TAKING STRATEGY

If you don't understand some words or ideas, you can still often get the general idea from the context. If you missed something important, put a ? in your notes and check with a classmate or the professor later.

F Predicting Content and Lecture Direction

Predicting the content and the direction of a lecture lets you organize your notes more effectively and listen more efficiently. It isn't necessary for predicting to always be correct in order for the skill to be useful for you, but your guesses should be reasonable ones.

Exercise 5

The following excerpt is from a sociology lecture about women and work. At 12 different points, you will be directed to stop reading and discuss with the class what you predict will come next. **Important:** Cover each section of the lecture until you are ready to read it. Don't read ahead until you have stopped and made a prediction!

All over the world the question of women's role in society is becoming ... or is an emotionally charged issue ... women are questioning their previous roles and exploring new roles ... everyone seems to have an opinion about it ... one good thing that has come out of this is that women now feel that they have control or more control over the direction of their lives ... but this has caused some conflict ... in fact ... some people are saying that there is more strain on women than ever before ... in any case ... at least in the United States and many other countries ... women must now decide a major question ...

Stop and Predict

Whether to work outside of the home ... pursue a career ... or whether to stay at home and raise a family or whether to do both ... I must add that this is the dilemma of a lucky few women ... here in the United States nowadays the majority of working women must work outside and it is no longer a luxury ... but anyway what I would like to focus on in this lecture are some of the factors a woman might want to take into account when deciding whether to enter the job market or not ...

Stop and Predict

A major question would be which one is emotionally and physically more beneficial ...

Stop and Predict

 *Let me first look at the physical side of the question …*

Stop and Predict

 *Previously we knew that men had a higher heart-attack rate than women did ... and that most people blamed that on the fact that they worked outside of the home and women didn't ... work in the job market being more stressful than staying at home ... however …*

Stop and Predict

 *Now with more than 50 percent of women in the job market and still there is an uneven heart-attack rate ... this theory has lost credibility ... in fact research has shown that women who work outside of the home appear to be at no greater risk than women who stay at home ... for heart disease at least ... so …*

Stop and Predict

 *It seems that physically there is no benefit … in working outside the home or not … they seem to be about equal … but ... what about the emotional side of the question?*

Stop and Predict

 *I'd like to tell you about a study that was done at three universities and colleges that compared women working in the job market to housewives … the employed women … whose mean age was 33 … ranged from secretaries to professionals and executives ... most of the women in both groups were college educated ... now the test was designed to study who was emotionally stronger ... the women in the job market or the housewives ... the researchers defined emotional strength as ... the degree ... of psychological distress … to which someone ... reacts … to a life crisis ... let me repeat that ... the degree ... of psychological distress … to which someone … reacts … to a life crisis … in other words how much psychological distress did they show when there was a crisis in their lives? … you might ask, well, how did the researchers judge psychological distress?*

Stop and Predict

 *They used five measures ... the first measure was anxiety ... how much anxiety did the woman report in her life? ... how often did she complain of anxiety? ... the second one ... irritability ... how often did she complain of being irritated? ... the third one ... somatic complaints ... somatic meaning bodily ... complaints relating to the body ... in other words ... how often did the woman complain about having headaches or backaches? ... the fourth one ... depression ... how often did the woman complain about being depressed? feeling depressed? ... the fifth one was problems in thinking and concentrating ... how often did the woman complain about having this sort of problem? ... added together these measures formed a way of judging how much psychological distress was in someone's life ... what did the researchers find? …*

Stop and Predict

 *First of all they found that housewives generally experience lower levels of stressful life events than employed women do ... yet ...*

Stop and Predict

 *They seem to react to life crises with more psychological distress than employed women do ... that is ...*

Stop and Predict

 *They have less stress in their lives yet they show more psychological distress ... to put it from the employed women's perspective ... the employed women have more stress in their lives both at work and in their marriages yet they show fewer signs of psychological distress ... this test seems to imply quite a lot ...*

Stop and Predict

 *It implies that employment may equip women better for coping with stressful life events than does staying at home ... the researchers caution that other factors such as social class ... job status ... may contribute to these differences ... and that the results may apply only to certain types of women in certain situations.*

How did you do? Were you able to predict the direction of the lecture at least some of the time? If so, that's good. Once again, predicting does not mean getting the right answer; it means making an educated guess.

LISTENING AND NOTE-TAKING STRATEGY

Use cues to organization and topic introduction to predict what the lecturer will cover. Predicting well helps you organize your notes as well as listen more effectively as an active, involved listener.

USING INTRODUCTIONS, CONCLUSIONS, AND DIGRESSIONS

I'm going to start out today by ...
and that will remind me of a story about ... which will remind me of the time ... which will remind me of a funny incident ...

Goals

- Use cues to introductions, conclusions, and digressions to take better notes
- Recognize a lecturer's direction and goals from introductions
- Confirm key points in conclusions

Discussion

Your Reactions to Lecturer Styles

1. What are some things that lecturers can do to make it easy for listeners to follow a lecture?
2. What is the function of introductions and conclusions in lectures? Do you usually take notes during these sections? Why or why not?
3. What are some reasons that lecturers digress while they are speaking? How do you recognize digressions? How do you know when they are finished?
4. Have you had professors who digress frequently? How did you and others react to those digressions?

Understanding Lecture Focus and Direction from Introductions

Lecturers might begin their lecture by doing one or more of these things:

- warm up with some introductory remarks
- introduce the main topic with some background information or general statements
- tell a personal story or joke to introduce the topic
- review or summarize material from a previous lecture or the textbook
- give an overview of the lecture plan and state the lecture or lesson goals

Listeners need to know when the introduction is finished and the body of the lecture, which contains the key points, begins.

LISTENING AND NOTE-TAKING STRATEGY

During the introduction, listen carefully to get a clear idea about the lecturer's goals. You don't usually need to take notes at this time. However, knowing the lecturer's organizational plan will make it easier for you to predict and take accurate notes during the body of the lecture.

CUES TO RECOGNIZE INTRODUCTIONS

1. Sentences giving an explicit overview of the lecture:

   I'd like to do three things today. Firstly, I'll give some background information about X. Then we'll look at the state of X today. Finally, we'll look at some work that is being carried out now and what it might mean for the future.

2. Sentences indicating a lecture's general focus:

   Today's lecture focuses on X.

3. Sentences or rhetorical questions referring to a continuation of a previous lecture:

   In our last class, we talked about X.
   What do you remember from last week?

Exercise 1

You will hear the beginnings of five different lectures. First, read the question about each excerpt. Then listen to the excerpt and answer the question.

Example

What will this lecture be about? Check (✓) all correct answers.

___ **a.** a history of romantic love

___ **b.** the reasons why romantic love fails

___ **c.** love's effects on the brain

___ **d.** gender differences in the experience of love

___ **e.** the future of love

The lecturer said:

I want to start with my work on romantic love because that's my most recent work. What I and my colleagues did was to put 32 people, who were madly in love, into a functional MRI brain scanner: 17 who were madly in love and their love was accepted. And 15 who were madly in love and they had just been dumped. And so I want to tell you about that first, and then go on into where I think "love" is going.[1]

The best answers are (c) and (e).

1. What will this psychology lecture be about? Check one.

   ___ **a.** reasons why positive psychology is so popular on college campuses

   ___ **b.** the controversies ("the storms") that positive psychology has created on campuses

   ___ **c.** the history of positive psychology and where it has evolved[2] from

   ___ **d.** a, b, and c

2. What will this biology lecture be about? Check one.

   ___ **a.** prenatal (before birth) development

   ___ **b.** physical growth from birth to adolescence (early teens)

   ___ **c.** emotional and physical growth from birth to adolescence

   ___ **d.** a and b

3. What will this sociology lecture be about? Check all correct answers.

   ___ **a.** the university's role in meeting Asian-American students' needs

   ___ **b.** a history of Asian immigration to the United States

   ___ **c.** the cultural and psychological characteristics of Asian-Americans in the United States

   ___ **d.** the present status of Asian-Americans in the United States

4. What will this lecture be about? Check all correct answers.

   ___ **a.** foreign policy in Latin America

   ___ **b.** the politics of education

   ___ **c.** doing library-based research

   ___ **d.** the process of looking for information

(continued on next page)

[1] Dr. Helen Fisher, Rutgers University, "The Science of Love and the Future of Women," TED Talk, February 2006

[2] ***evolve:*** to develop (often gradually or in stages)

5. What is the primary purpose of this ecology[1] lecture? Check one.

___ a. to give students a *reasoned* and *emotional* approach to the relationship between the human species and its environment

___ b. to give students a *reasoned* approach to the relationship between the human species and its environment

___ c. to give students an *emotional* approach to the relationship between the human species and its environment

___ d. to give students an overview of programs available on educational TV about ecology

Using Conclusions to Check the Lecture's Main Points

LISTENING AND NOTE-TAKING STRATEGY

Listen to the conclusion to check that you noted down all key points. Note any predictions, recommendations, or calls to action.

Although sometimes lecturers may simply run out of time and end abruptly, often lecturers sum up their talks with a conclusion that does one or more of these things:

- restates the lecture's key points
- connects different aspects of the topic
- discusses the topic's consequences
- makes a prediction about the future
- recommends a course of action or opinion

A review or a generalization gives the listeners the opportunity to double-check their notes and make sure that they reflect what the lecturer thought was important.

CUES TO RECOGNIZE CONCLUSIONS

1. Phrases signaling a forthcoming summary, logical conclusion, or ending:

   As we can see,

   This brings us to...

   Therefore, ...

   To sum up (in a few words), ...

   In conclusion, ...

   So in the final analysis...

   The bottom line here is ...

   What I'd like you to get from this is...

   The take-away here is that...

---

[1] *ecology:* the science that deals with the interrelationships between organisms and their environment

2. Words or phrases that tie together previously stated ideas:

For (all of) these reasons, …	***These examples (serve to) show …***
So what can we conclude from this?	***What we've learned from this is that…***
All of this adds up to…	***What all this proves is …***

Exercise 2

You will hear the conclusions of five different lectures. First, read the question about each excerpt. Then listen to the excerpt and answer the questions.

Example:
What did this lecture on sleep, memory, and dreams cover? Check all correct answers.

___ **a.** physiological brain changes throughout the night

___ **b.** chemical brain changes through the night

___ **c.** the effect of sleep on memories

___ **d.** the role of dreams in brain changes and memory processing

The lecturer said:

So I want to leave you with just some summary statements … that the physiology and chemistry of the brain change dramatically across the night…. that sleep consolidates and enhances memory…. that it changes the way that associative memories are processed as you're doing this work during the night … and that dreams are part of the story.[1]

Therefore, all of the answers are correct.

Did you know?

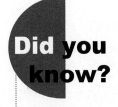

Teens need at least 8.5 to 9.25 hours of sleep each night, compared to an average of 7 to 9 hours each night for most adults.

1. This is from a lecture on race relations in U.S. history. What has the lecturer already talked about? Check all correct answers.

   ___ **a.** the role of the President

   ___ **b.** the role of the Supreme Court

   ___ **c.** the role of state governments

   ___ **d.** the role of Congress

   What will the lecturer talk about next? Check one.

   ___ **a.** the role of the President

   ___ **b.** the role of the Supreme Court

   ___ **c.** the role of state governments

   ___ **d.** the role of Congress

[1] Dr. Robert Stickgold, Harvard Medical School, "Sleep, Memory, and Dreams: What Are They Good For?" Irvine Health Foundation Lecture Series, March 16, 2004

2. This is from a lecture about nineteenth-century U.S. history. The lecturer previously listed many ways that blacks and whites were segregated (i.e., racially separated) in the South, including a discussion of separate seating areas on public transportation. He concludes by asking, "What was the point of all this?"

   What *was* the "point," according to the lecturer? ____________________

   When the lecturer finishes the conclusion, there is a cue to a new topic introduction ("Okay ... another area ... an important area ..."). What will the lecturer speak about next? ________________________________

3. This is from a lecture about paleoanthropology (the study of human evolutionary history). What does the lecturer *most* want students to understand? Check one.

   ___ **a.** why there was confusion in paleoanthropology prior to 1950

   ___ **b.** why Homo Erectus (an early human species) lasted so long

   ___ **c.** why Homo Erectus did so well

   ___ **d.** why paleoanthropology was so important prior to 1950

4. This is from a lecture on memory. The lecturer quotes a writer, Jane Austen, who thinks that memory is so mysterious that we'll never figure it out. What is the lecturer's opinion of that idea? Check all correct answers.

   ___ **a.** She agrees with Austen and believes that memory will never be understood.

   ___ **b.** She thinks Austen is too pessimistic[1] about our failure to understand memory.

   ___ **c.** She thinks that we have made progress in understanding memory.

   ___ **d.** She thinks there's hope to understand memory more in the future.

5. This was a lecture about *autism*, a disease in which people have difficulty communicating and interacting with others around them. What point(s) did the lecturer make in the conclusion about autism? Check all correct answers.

   ___ **a.** Autism is a devastating[2] disorder, and people with autism experience difficulty in the world.

   ___ **b.** We don't understand people with autism, and they don't understand us, so there is a communication problem both ways.

   ___ **c.** Autism might be a cognitive style (that is, a way of thinking) and not a deficit (that is, an insufficiency).

   ___ **d.** Scientists' goals should be to change that cognitive style.

---

[1] ***pessimistic:*** looking on the negative side of things

[2] ***devastating:*** overwhelming, powerful (emotionally or physically), capable of causing destruction

C Digressions

Speakers digress more frequently than writers. A digression can be intentional, such as an interesting story, a joke, or an important piece of information that suddenly comes to mind; or unintentional, such as when speakers go from one point to another and eventually find themselves far from the intended topic.

You need to recognize digressions so that they do not confuse you and distract you from the key points of the lecture. They also might provide a break from continuous note-taking.

Although digressions are sometimes preceded by specific cues ("That reminds me of a funny story ..."), more often they are not. However, cues are often used *after* a digression to bring the audience back to the original subject.

LISTENING AND NOTE-TAKING STRATEGY

Use digressions as an opportunity to take a break from active note-taking. Pay attention to cues that signal a return to the main lecture topic.

CUES TO RECOGNIZE DIGRESSIONS

1. Phrases or sentences signaling a possible digression:

   Now, before I go on, ...

   Now, this brings to mind...

   By the way, did I ever tell you about...

   This might be a little off-track, but...

   Speaking of X, ...

   That reminds me of a story.

2. Words or phrases following a digression:

   Now, let's see, where were we?

   (Well) anyway, ...

   But getting back to (what we were talking about), ...

   I seem to have gotten off track ...

   At any rate, ...

3. Rhetorical questions following a digression and signaling a return to the original subject:

   Now, what were we talking about?

   Where did we stop?

   Now, where did we leave off?

Exercise 3

You will hear five lecture excerpts. First, read the questions about each excerpt. Then listen without taking notes. After listening, answer these questions about each excerpt:

- What is the digression?
- Would this information be important to note?

1. In the main part of this lecture on the spread of disease, the speaker talks about how a specific plague—the bubonic plague—typically spreads.

   VOCABULARY

   plague: a quickly spreading, infectious, dangerous disease

2. In the main part of this lecture on family systems, the speaker describes the three types of marriage payments: bride price, dowry, and bride service.

   VOCABULARY

   kin: relatives
   vestige: evidence of something that no longer exists

3. In the main part of this lecture on anthropology and how to date fossils and other materials, the speaker tells about *taphonomy*, the study of decaying organisms over time, and its importance in *forensic anthropology*, a branch of physical anthropology in which anthropological data and techniques are used to investigate crimes.

   VOCABULARY

   corpse: dead body
   decay: decomposition; reduction in quality or health
   coroner: an officer whose function is to investigate unusual deaths

4. In the main part of this geology lecture, the speaker tells about the oldest living trees on the planet, bristlecone pines.

5. In the main part of this zoology lecture on animal communication, the speaker tells about kinds of pheromones, chemical substances that animals use to communicate with each other. One kind of pheromone, the *aggregation* pheromone, is used to call members of the species together.

Did you know?

The bubonic plague killed approximately one-third of Europe's population during a three-year period (1347-1350).

Exercise 4

Listen to the five excerpts in Exercise 3 again. Pause after each one and discuss whether the lecturer signaled the beginning or end of the digression. For example, did the lecturer use any cues, change his or her tone of voice, or simply change the topic?

NOTE-TAKING BASICS

4

Goals

- Choose key words to note
- Use abbreviations and symbols in notes
- Visually represent the relative importance of information
- Visually represent the relationship between pieces of information

DISCUSSION

Note-Taking

1. When you take notes in your native language, do you try to write down every word? If you don't, how do you decide what to write down? Do you do the same in English? Why or why not?

2. How often do you review your notes after a lecture? Do you add information? Do you change information?

3. What are some advantages to comparing your notes with other students? Are there any disadvantages?

4. What are some advantages to recording your lectures? Are there any disadvantages or difficulties? If you record your lectures, how soon do you listen to them again? Do you take notes at that time, or check notes that you took before?

Recognizing and Using Key Words

Because you don't have time to write down every word a speaker says, you want to concentrate on noting the key words, words that carry the most meaning.

Notice how key words are noted in the following example.

LECTURER: *Mount Everest is the highest mountain in the world ... that's why everyone wants to climb it ... you're on the roof of the world ...*

NOTES: Mt. Everest – highest mountain in world

Notice how the verb *to be* and articles (*a/an* and *the*) are not important and don't need to be noted. As mentioned earlier, paraphrases and repetitions indicate important ideas, but don't need to be noted more than once. Digressions are not usually important to note.

As a general rule, nouns, active verbs, and adjectives are key words. However, choosing key words to note also greatly depends on the context. Most often, for example, prepositions are not key words. In the following example, the preposition "on" is unimportant.

LECTURER: *Gandhi was assassinated on January 30, 1948.*

NOTES: Gandhi assassinated 1/30/48.

However, in the following case, the preposition "on" *is* a key word.

LECTURER: *A cataract is a cloudiness of the eye's lens that typically prevents light from forming a clear image on the retina.*

NOTES: cataract—eye lens cloudiness—no clear image on retina

USUALLY KEY WORDS	NOT USUALLY KEY WORDS
• **nouns**, especially names and dates *(Marie Curie, 1492, volcanoes)* • **active verbs** *(invented, fought, destroyed)* • **adjectives** and **adverbs**, especially comparatives and superlatives *(high, least contagious)*	• pronouns *(we, they)* • the verb **be** (*was, is*) • prepositions *(over, in, at, to)* • articles (*a, an, the*) • repeated words or paraphrases *(beautiful, gorgeous, spectacular)* • digressions *(That reminds me of the time my father took me to the circus ...)*

NOTE-TAKING STRATEGY

Note key words, instead of trying to write everything the speaker says. Be concise with your note-taking. Do not worry about grammar or spelling.

B Making Abbreviations Work for You

Your notes need to make sense to you after the lecture—sometimes as much as a week or even several months later. For this reason, be careful with abbreviations.

LECTURER: *New York City was the capital of the U.S. until 1790.*

NOTES: NYC-capital U.S. till 1790

"NYC" are initials that are familiar to most Americans, so it makes sense to use them. Compare the following two sets of notes.

LECTURER: *New Orleans was established in 1718 as a colony by the French.*

GOOD NOTES: New Orleans estab. 1718 by French

POOR NOTES: NO estab. 1718 by French

What is wrong with the second example? The initials "NO" are not familiar, and you would probably not know what they refer to if you read your notes later. However, you would probably recognize "estab." as an abbreviation for "established."

NOTE-TAKING STRATEGY

Choose abbreviations that you will be able to understand even much later.

C Using Note-Taking Symbols and Abbreviations

Symbols can replace words that show relationships. For example, the dash (—) can symbolize *was* or any other form of *to be.*

Example

George Washington — 1st U.S. Pres. = George Washington was the first President of the United States.

Exercise 1

Write the symbol or abbreviation you would use for these ideas. Then share your list with a partner.

_____ equals
_____ does not equal
_____ and
_____ is more than
_____ is less than
_____ money
_____ to go up; to increase
_____ to go down; to decrease
_____ leading to; heading toward
_____ therefore; so
_____ because
_____ inches / centimeters
_____ feet / meters
_____ degree
_____ at
_____ Pay attention!

_____ per (as in *10 per thousand*)
_____ approximately; about
_____ since 1929
_____ 1929 and earlier
_____ century
_____ with
_____ without
_____ man; men
_____ woman; women
_____ for example
_____ (repeated words)
_____ number
_____ that is; in other words
_____ percent
_____ plus; in addition to

Do you use any other symbols? Share them with the class. Note any additional symbols that you would like to remember in the space below.

Exercise 2

You will hear ten statements. Take notes in as few words as possible, using symbols and abbreviations where you can. Then compare your notes in small groups.

> **NOTE-TAKING STRATEGY**
>
> Develop your own symbols and abbreviations that are meaningful and useful to you.

Example

LECTURER: *As women in developing countries get more education, family size in that group tends to go down.*

NOTES: ♀ in developing countries: when education ↑, family size ↓

1.

2.

3.

4. Worlds comp using Men > Woman
21% of pop'n use comp in India
♂ dbl ♀ use a comp

5.
TV average American watches 3h 46 min / day
52 days/year lots TV programs

6.
Huge continent Antarctica 5.5 mil m^2
14.2 mil km^2 Summer size Australia 50 size uk

7. In winter the ice changes double in size of antarctica

8. Mercury: a planet in solar system
near to the Sun, smallest in the 8 planets

9. One of the biggest things happened in 20th cent.
First man on the Moon 1969 July 20 Neil Armstrong
2 min 32 s on the moon

10.
Blue whale biggest mammal pop'n of 275 000
now less than 5000 reduction due to uncontrol hunting

Visually Representing Relationships and the Relative Importance of Information

Use the space on your paper and write your notes in such a way as to show relationships and the relative importance of information at a glance.

Example

LECTURER: *There are three important learning styles to consider … and each one of us has preferences or tendencies to learn better using certain styles … those three styles are visual … auditory … and kinesthetic … And let me give you examples of each one … if you tend toward a visual learning style, you like to* <u>see</u> *things … you learn best through visual means … reading … viewing a movie … If you tend toward an auditory learning style, you like to* <u>hear</u> *things.… You excel at listening to instructions, listening to lectures.… And if you have a kinesthetic style, you learn by* <u>moving</u> *or* <u>doing</u> *… you do better when you can do something hands-on … a lab experiment for example …*

NOTES: 3 learning styles:
visual—seeing, e.g. read, movie
auditory—hearing, e.g. listen to lecture
kinesthetic—moving/doing, e.g. hands-on lab

OR

NOTES:

3 learning styles

visual	auditory	kinesthetic
Seeing	Listening	Moving/doing
e.g. read, movie	e.g. listen to lecture	e.g. hands-on labs

The arrangement of both sets of notes clearly shows how information relates to the particular topic; that is, the notes show the three learning styles with information about each one. The second set, in particular, visually reflects the lecture organization.

You can also indent information to indicate its relative importance. Write the most general information farthest to the left. Write more specific information under the general information and indent it to the right.

Example

LECTURER: *A poll was taken recently surveying 1200 adults in the United States to find out what they considered important in their lives. Ninety-six percent said that having a good family life was important. Ninety-five percent said that using their mind and abilities was important. This latter quality was most important to women beginning work careers. This priority marks a shift in the type of work people are involved in—moving away from physical labor and toward jobs requiring mental skills.*

NOTES: poll—1,200 Americans—What is important in your life?

96%—have good family life

95%—use mind and abilities

most important to ♀ beginning careers

shows shift in work habits → jobs requiring mental skills, not physical labor

There are other ways to arrange this information into notes. In all cases, make sure that you use as few words as possible and accurately express the lecturer's ideas in terms of relative importance of information and relationship between pieces of information.

NOTE-TAKING STRATEGY

Design your notes so that you can easily see which information is the most important and to show how ideas are related to one another.

Exercise 3

You will hear ten short statements. Take informative notes in as few words as possible on a separate sheet of paper. Use symbols, abbreviations, key words, indentation, and connecting lines where appropriate. When you have finished, compare your notes in a small group.

1.

2.

3.

LECTURE 2

Women and Work (Sociology)

In Unit 2, you practiced predicting content and lecture direction while reading a transcript of a lecture on women and work. Now listen to the entire lecture. While listening, look at the following example notes.

Major ? — ♀ work outside? stay home? both?

Which is emotionally and physically more beneficial?

study— 3 univ. & colleges
compare employed ♀ & housewives
  mean age 33
  sec'y & prof.
  most college ed.
designed to see who was emotionally stronger

in past, ♂ had higher heart-attack rate perhaps because worked outside?

BUT — now 50+% ♀ in jobs & still uneven rate

<u>Emotional strength:</u> degree of psych distress to which someone reacts to a life crisis

∴ NO BENEFIT in work outside or not (about =)

How judge?
1. anxiety
2. irritability
3. somatic (body) complaints
4. depression
5. problems in thinking & concentrating

Results?
Housewives — ↓ levels of stress in lives YET react to crises w/ ↑ distress
Employed ♀ — ↑ stress in lives YET show ↓ distress

Implies?
employment equips ♀ for coping w/ stress better

(Results may apply to only some ♀, not all)

Did you notice the following?

- The notes visually represent the organization of the lecture and the relative importance of pieces of information in the lecture.
- The major points are written farthest to the left, with details indented under the generalizations that they support.
- The major issue—whether work outside the home is emotionally or physically beneficial or harmful to women—stands out. There is information about the emotional side of the problem in one area of the page and information about the physical side of the problem in another.
- Headings such as "Results?" and "Implies?" help to organize the notes by clarifying the purpose of important sections.

E Note-Taking Practice

Listen to the lecture again. Without looking back at the example, take notes on a separate sheet of paper. Use symbols, abbreviations, key words, indentation, connecting lines, and headings where appropriate.

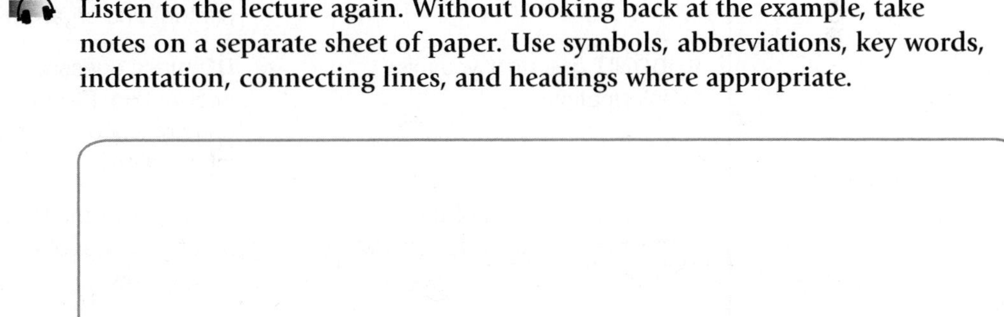

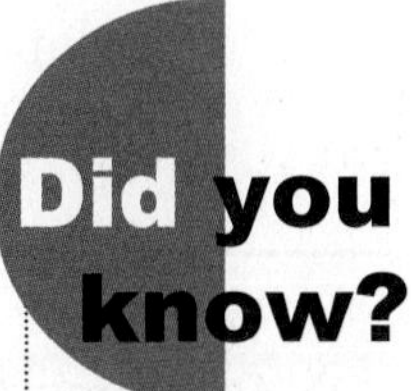

Did you know?

In the United States, between 1965 and 2003, men tripled the amount of time they spent caring for children.

Eight DOs and DON'Ts for Improving Lecture Comprehension and Note-Taking

1. **DON'T** note every word.	**DO** note key words. Remember that nouns, active verbs, and adjectives are usually most important.
2. **DON'T** write complete words.	**DO** use abbreviations and symbols.
3. **DON'T** note indiscriminately.	**DO** evaluate as you listen. Decide what is important and what is not.
4. **DON'T** take notes as if you were writing a composition.	**DO** use the space on your paper to organize information and visually represent the relationship between ideas.
5. **DON'T** be a passive listener.	**DO** be an active listener. Predict lecture content and organization.
6. **DON'T** give up if you miss information.	**DO** make guesses if you miss information. Remember that lecturers usually repeat and paraphrase information.
7. **DON'T** lose sight of the forest for the trees. (Don't listen for details before getting the larger picture.)	**DO** listen for the lecturer's main points and for the general organizational framework.
8. **DON'T** forget about your notes when you leave the lecture.	**DO** rewrite and/or revise your notes as soon as possible after the lecture. That way, ideas that you did not have time to note will still be fresh in your mind and you will be able to add them. In addition, you can reorganize information so that the ideas are more clearly and accurately represented.

Do you have any other DOs or DON'Ts for improving lecture comprehension and note-taking to recommend? Share your ideas with your classmates.

NOTING NUMBERS AND STATISTICS EFFECTIVELY

Goals

- Accurately note large numbers, fractions, decimals, ratios, and dates
- Accurately note numbers, dates, and statistics and their significance while listening to lectures

DISCUSSION

Numbers

1. What academic subjects have you studied (or do you expect to study) that use a lot of numbers? What kinds of numbers are typically mentioned in lectures in that field (e.g., ages, measurements, dates, statistics, fractions, decimals, percentages, ratios, equations)?
2. What kinds of numbers are easy for you to comprehend and note? What kinds of numbers are challenging and why? How do you usually note numbers—in words? figures? Is it easy for you to understand your notes later?
3. Talk about five key dates in the history of your native country (or another country that you know well). Why are those dates so important?
4. What percentage of your classmates have a pet? Live by themselves? Read the newspaper everyday? Grew up in a rural area? Voted in the past year? Make a guess and then take a survey to find out the reality. Make up three additional questions to survey.
5. Discuss an interesting survey or research study from your field of interest.

A Numbers: A Review

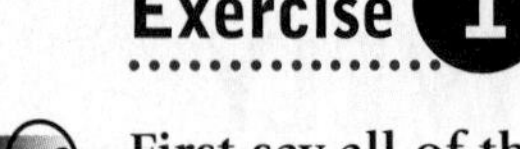

Exercise 1

First say all of the numbers out loud. Then listen and circle the numbers that you hear.

1.	19	90	9	
2.	18	80	8	
3.	13	30	33	
4.	205	250	2,005	
5.	6,000,250	625,000	6,250,000	
6.	18	180	1,080	
7.	83,000	80,300	803,000	
8.	2,758	2,758,000	2,700,058	
9.	7,000,040	7,000,400	7,000,040,000	
10.	5,020	5,200	52,000	
11.	$\frac{4}{5}$	45	$4\frac{1}{5}$	4.5
12.	$\frac{5}{8}$	58	$5\frac{1}{8}$	5.8
13.	$\frac{1}{5}$	105	$1\frac{1}{5}$	1.5
14.	$\frac{2}{8}$	208	$2\frac{1}{8}$	2.8

Exercise 2

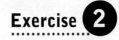

You will hear twelve numbers. Write the numbers that you hear.

1. ______ 5. ______ 9. ______
2. ______ 6. ______ 10. ______
3. ______ 7. ______ 11. ______
4. ______ 8. ______ 12. ______

Exercise 3

You will hear five ratios or proportions. Write the numbers that you hear.

1. In Lesotho in 2005, an estimated ______ adults lived with HIV/AIDS.
2. By 2030, Africa and Asia will account for almost ______ urban inhabitants globally.
3. In Burkina Faso in 2003, more than ______ children under 5 had iron-deficiency anemia.
4. In India in 2005, men used computers at home or at work more than women did, ______.
5. In the United States in 2007, the number of infant deaths was ______.

LECTURE 3

Milestones in Technology (History/Technology)

Vocabulary

Related to Inventions

Check (✓) the words you know. Underline the words you want to learn. Then check their meaning with your instructor or in a dictionary.

to discover
to design
to invent
to devise
to develop

to patent
a patent

an innovation
a breakthrough

creativity
imagination
ingeniousness
ingenuity
inventiveness
originality

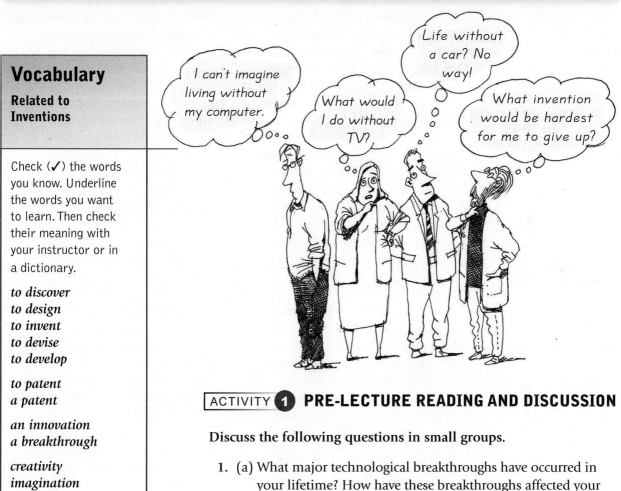

ACTIVITY 1 PRE-LECTURE READING AND DISCUSSION

Discuss the following questions in small groups.

1. (a) What major technological breakthroughs have occurred in your lifetime? How have these breakthroughs affected your life and the lives of those around you?

   (b) What ten inventions would you have the hardest time living without?

2. If you were a CEO (chief executive officer) or a manager and wanted to encourage employee creativity and innovation, what would you do? (For example, would you offer employees incentives for new ideas? Would you give employees time to daydream?) Think of three ways you might encourage creativity in your company.

3. Read the following article from *Newsweek* magazine. Discuss the techniques that some large corporations—such as Du Pont, Pfizer, 3M, and Bell Labs—use to encourage creativity. Would you like to work under these conditions? Why or why not?

The Houses of Invention

If the great inventions of the past were usually the work of an individual—a Gutenberg, an Edison, a Bell—then those of the twentieth century are increasingly the brainchildren of entire labs. In an age marked by an explosion of knowledge, argues Warren Bennis of the University of Southern California, "one is too small a number to produce greatness." Some solitary[1] inventors notwithstanding,[2] America's engines of invention are corporate labs. What makes a great one?

At Du Pont, it takes up to 250 ideas to generate[3] one major, marketable new product. At Pfizer Inc., the yield is one new drug out of 100 possibilities. All of the ultimate losers suck up[4] money before the winner pays off. Success therefore requires taking "monetary risks that would give most corporate finance officers a case of indigestion," says management guru[5] Tom Peters.

At 3M, the rule is that 30 percent of sales must come from products less than four years old. And its scientists and engineers can spend up to five percent of company time on their own projects, without even telling managers what they're up to.[6] Both policies send a clear signal that risk-taking is a core[7] value. Du Pont researchers may pursue their blue-sky ideas[8] one day a week. The idea is to be open to serendipity:[9] every scientist makes mistakes, but only in a culture that encourages the exploration of the unknown do you get Teflon[10] (when a Du Pont scientist working on Freon accidentally polymerized several gases into a white powder). "A universal characteristic of innovative[11] companies is an open culture," says Rosabeth Moss Kanter of Harvard Business School.

In a corporate lab, the walls between chemists and physicists, metallurgists and mechanics are often lower than in academe.[12] It was by throwing together physicists with metallurgists and chemists that Bell Labs wove together[13] the diverse talents that invented the transistor.[14] Says William Brinkman, vice president for physical-sciences research at Bell Labs, "We call it 'spontaneous[15] teaming'—you see an interesting problem that another group is working on and you want to be part of it."

[1] ***solitary:*** lone, single
[2] ***notwithstanding:*** not included
[3] ***generate:*** to yield, to produce
[4] ***suck up:*** to consume; to use up
[5] ***guru:*** teacher or expert (often spiritual)
[6] ***be up to:*** to be involved in
[7] ***core:*** key, central
[8] ***blue-sky ideas:*** fantasies; idealistic ideas
[9] ***serendipity:*** chance
[10] ***Teflon:*** a well-known nonstick product (used on pans)
[11] ***innovative:*** relating to new ideas
[12] ***academe:*** higher education
[13] ***weave together:*** to interconnect pieces
[14] ***transistor:*** an electronic part that controls the flow of electricity in a machine
[15] ***spontaneous:*** occurring without prior planning

ACTIVITY 2 PREPARING FOR THE LECTURE

The title of the lecture is "Milestones in Technology." What do you expect the lecturer to tell you in the lecture? Brainstorm ideas with your classmates.

 **Listen to the beginning of the lecture. Notice that the lecturer is very interactive, encouraging students to participate. The lecturer refers to a handout with this definition of technology:**

Technology

1a. The application of science, esp. to industrial or commercial objectives.
1b. The entire body of methods and materials used to achieve such objectives.
2. *Anthropol.* The body of knowledge available to a civilization that is of use in fashioning implements, practicing manual arts and skills, and extracting or collecting materials.

1. What point is the lecturer trying to make in the classroom discussion about the definitions of "technology"?
   ___ **a.** Technology is always related to science.
   ___ **b.** Technology is always related to commerce.
   ___ **c.** Technology is always related to science, but not necessarily related to commerce
   ___ **d.** Technology doesn't need to be related to either commerce or science.

2. "Technology" can mean different things. When the lecturer uses the word in this lecture, which definition from the above box will he be using?
   ___ **a.** the first definition (1a and 1b)
   ___ **b.** the second definition
   ___ **c.** both definitions
   ___ **d.** neither definition; a new one

3. The lecturer is going to talk about "milestones in the history of technology." How far back in time does he plan to go back?
   ___ **a.** decades
   ___ **b.** hundreds of years ("centuries")
   ___ **c.** thousands of years ("millennia")
   ___ **d.** millions of years

ACTIVITY 3 LISTENING AND NOTING

You will hear a lecture about millions of years of technology, highlighting milestone events and their dates. Complete the following chart with the dates, technological breakthroughs, and locations (if mentioned). The definition of "technology" is on page 45.

DATE	TECHNOLOGICAL BREAKTHROUGH	LOCATION
2,400,000 B.C.	stone tools	
1.000.000 BC	ancestors began to control fire	
90.000 BC	bone points	Africa
25.000 BC	began weaving cloth	
23.000 BC	used bow & arrow	
10.000 BC	first known pa	Japan
5.000 B.C	started mining copper	Egypt
? 35 hun. BC	wild wickles	Syria
2.000 BC	first interie bathrooms	Greece
? 15 hun BC	earliest glass vessels	Egypt
? 1 hun 40 BC	make paper	China
100 BC	water used to power mills	East. Europe
A.D. 600	first wild builds	Iran
100 '	gun powder	China
	Developed movable type for printing	China
1608	first telescope	Holland

Indust. Rev—tech. proceeding at incredible speed:
e.g., tech esp. relevant to students

Conclusions: course of discovery
come a long way from stone tools

ACTIVITY 4 REPLAY QUESTION

Listen to this section of the lecture. The professor says, "pun intended." A "pun" is a verbal joke, a play on words. What is the professor's pun?

____

LISTENING AND NOTE-TAKING STRATEGY

Ask classmates for information that you missed: "Excuse me, I didn't catch the date for the invention of photocopying. Do you have that in your notes?" Or ask your teacher: "Excuse me. Could you repeat the date for the invention of photocopying?"

ACTIVITY 5 "OTHER VOICES" FOLLOW-UP

Following the lecture, there is a class discussion about creativity and innovation. Listen and then answer the questions.

1. Why does the professor tell a joke?

   ___ **a.** He wants to make a point about the characteristics of creative people.

   ___ **b.** He's digressing from the main point about creativity and entertaining the class.

   ___ **c.** He's making a point about the relationship between religion and creativity.

   ___ **d.** He wants to make a point that all children are naturally creative.

2. What quality did the little girl NOT exhibit?

   ___ **a.** perseverance[1] when facing others' doubt

   ___ **b.** faith (i.e., belief, trust) in herself

   ___ **c.** drawing talent

   ___ **d.** fearlessness

3. What question does the professor conclude with?

   How can our classrooms and businesses ______________________________?

4. Sometimes it is important to take notes during a class discussion, especially when the professor emphasizes certain points. Listen to this discussion again and note the important information on a separate sheet of paper.

---

[1] ***perseverance:*** continued and persistent effort to reach a goal

ACTIVITY 6 USING YOUR NOTES

STUDY STRATEGY

Successful students often work in study groups to review material, asking and answering questions that are likely to be on tests.

Write 10 questions with *who, what, where,* or *when* about the information in this lecture. Use a separate sheet of paper.

Example
Who invented gunpowder?
When did people begin weaving cloth?
What happened in 90,000 B.C.?

Work in groups of three. Test each other, referring back to your notes when necessary, with your 10 questions. If you disagree about any answers, listen to the lecture section again or ask for clarification.

ACTIVITY 7 POST-LECTURE DISCUSSION

Discuss the following questions in small groups.

1. The lecturer names several inventions from after the Industrial Revolution. Which ones do you consider to be true milestones when examined from a perspective covering many thousands of years of technological advances?

2. Look at this prediction about the fashion industry, published in the World Future Society's *Outlook 2008* report:

   Fashion will go wired[1] *as technologies and tastes … revolutionize the textile industry. Researchers in smart fabrics and intelligent textiles (SFIT) are working with the fashion industry to bring us color-changing or perfume-emitting*[2] *jeans … and running shoes … that watch where you're going (possibly allowing others to do the same). Powering these gizmos*[3] *remains a key obstacle.*[4] *But industry watchers estimate that a $400 million market for SFIT is already in place and predict that smart fabrics could revitalize*[5] *the U.S. and European textile industry.* (Patrick Tucker, "Smart Fashion," *The Futurist*, September-October 2007, p. 68)

   Do you agree that this will happen over the next 25 years in the fashion industry?

   Think about other fields (e.g., agriculture, music, medicine, education) and make forecasts about likely technological innovations in the next 25 years.

3. Do you believe that some areas of technological research and development should be limited or prohibited? If so, which ones? Why?

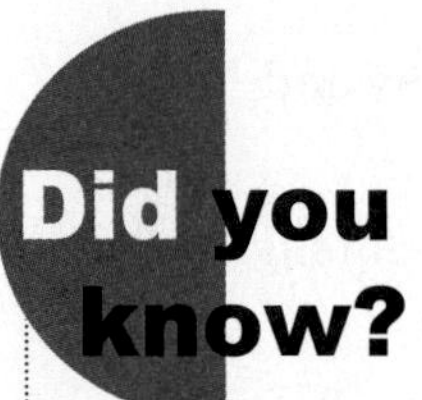

The saying "Necessity is the mother of invention" came from Plato, a Greek philosopher of the 4th century, B.C.E.

---

[1] ***go wired:*** to become high-tech; to become Internet-capable
[2] ***emit:*** to release
[3] ***gizmo:*** (informal) gadget; small, handy tool
[4] ***obstacle:*** a barrier preventing progress
[5] ***revitalize:*** to reenergize; to give new life to

ACTIVITY 8 ACADEMIC WORD LIST VOCABULARY[1]

Match the word to its meaning. Write the correct letter in the space provided. Examples are given to help you see words in context.

Group 1

a. a highly unusual event that attracts attention
b. a tool or implement
c. a continued and connected series
d. a machine that travels to transport people or things

____ 1. ***device*** The car is equipped with a device that measures tire pressure.

____ 2. ***vehicle*** The Department of Motor Vehicles can issue a driver's license to you.

____ 3. ***sequence*** A sequence of events led to the current situation.

____ 4. ***phenomenon*** A shooting star is a natural phenomenon, but it seems magical to me.

Group 2

a. to depend on
b. to remove; to pull out
c. to go forward or move ahead
d. to completely change

____ 5. ***extract*** How do miners extract minerals from the rock?

____ 6. ***proceed*** Let's proceed with the examination. I apologize for the interruption.

____ 7. ***rely on*** We can't always rely on cell phones in mountainous areas.

____ 8. ***revolutionize*** Computers revolutionized the way we work.

(continued on next page)

[1] The Academic Word List was developed in 2000 by Averil Coxhead from written material used in the fields of liberal arts, commerce, law, and science. Familiarity with the most common words from this list will help you better understand the language that you encounter in classes and textbooks. The words in this exercise come from the lecture you just heard. Throughout this book, additional words from the Academic Word List are marked with an asterisk (*).

Group 3

a. related or closely connected (to a matter)
b. done by hand (rather than machine)
c. clear; easy to see or understand
d. primary, main, most important

____	9. *manual*	The computer requires the manual input of data.
____	10. *relevant*	That information wasn't relevant to the audience, so I didn't include it in the presentation.
____	11. *major*	The major industry in that area is mining.
____	12. *obvious*	The answer is obvious: two plus two equals four!

ACTIVITY 9 USING VOCABULARY

Read the following conversation between a manager and employee. Fill in the blanks with the vocabulary in the box.

imagination	*proceed*	*relevant*
revolutionary	*turning point*	

Manager: How's the project going?

Employee: We were having a hard time with it, but I think we reached a ________________ (1.) yesterday.

Manager: What happened?

Employee: We were trying to figure out how to market this new color-changing fabric. We want consumers to see it as something ________________ (2.); that is, something completely different. Our minds were blank. I encouraged my coworkers to use their ________________ (3.), but they were stuck.

Manager: And then?

Employee: And then someone brought in an article about how color can affect moods and we all realized that this article was ________________ (4.) to our marketing plan. If we can convince consumers that colors affect them deeply, interest in our product will grow.

Manager: It sounds like you're heading in the right direction. ________________ (5.)!

 **Listen to the conversation to check your answers.**

ACTIVITY 10 RETAINING VOCABULARY

VOCABULARY LEARNING STRATEGY

Learners understand more vocabulary than they regularly use. Active vocabulary learners decide which words are important for production—not just reception—and practice those words in written and/or spoken contexts.

Write at least five words from the lecture, reading, or discussion that you would like to be able to use in speaking or writing. Write questions using those words on a separate sheet of paper and then ask your classmates your questions.

Example
turning point: What was a turning point in your life?

ACTIVITY 11 BEYOND THE LECTURE: SPEAKING AND LISTENING

What machine would you like to see invented—for example, a machine to remember your dreams? an exercise machine that works while you sleep? Work with a partner to design an invention. Think about who might use the invention, what it would do, how it would work, why it would be helpful, and how much it should cost. Then design an advertisement for your invention. When you have finished, present your invention and your advertisement to your classmates. Use the picture below and chart on the next page as examples to help plan and organize your presentation.

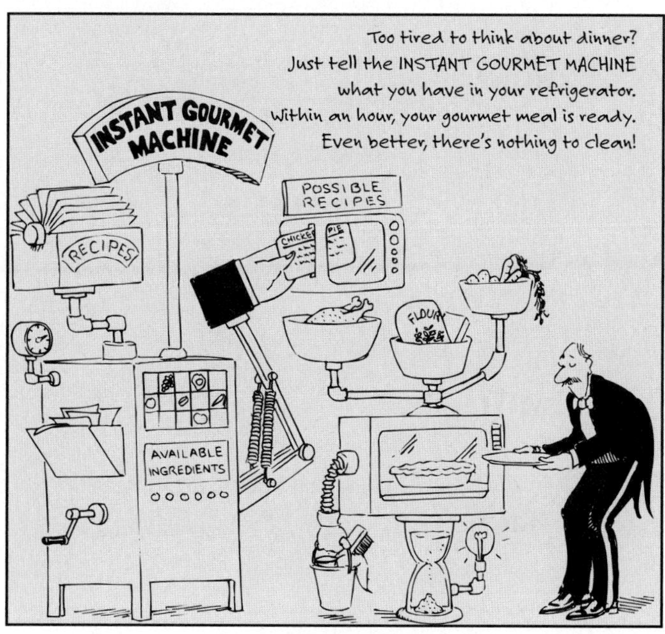

INVENTION: Instant Gourmet Machine

WHO? People with busy lives who don't enjoy cooking.

WHAT? A machine with an extensive database of thousands of recipes, compartments for ingredients, and cooking and cleaning abilities.

HOW?
1. Program in the foods that are in the kitchen.
2. The Instant Gourmet Machine (IGM) provides a selection of possible recipes.
3. Choose a recipe and place each ingredient in a separate compartment.
4. The IGM cooks the dish and signals when the food is ready.
5. The IGM cleans itself automatically.

WHY? It can save people time and energy, so they have more time to do the things they enjoy!

PRICE: $5,000

INVENTION:

WHO?

WHAT?

HOW?

WHY?

PRICE:

LECTURE 4

Immigration to the United States (History/Sociology)

Vocabulary

Related to Immigration

Check (✓) the words you know. Underline the words you want to learn. Then check their meaning with your instructor or in a dictionary.

to immigrate
to emigrate

ancestry
ancestor

descendant

ethnicity
ethnic diversity

to blend in
to assimilate

to retain one's identity

to seek refuge/asylum

to flee
to escape

persecution
oppression

melting pot

ACTIVITY 1 PRE-LECTURE READING AND DISCUSSION

Discuss the following questions in small groups.

1. The following excerpt is from a poem that is inscribed on the base of the Statue of Liberty. It was written by Emma Lazarus in 1883 to express her belief that the Statue of Liberty could be the "Mother of Exiles"[1] and that it would welcome all to its shores, especially the tired, the poor, and those whom other countries didn't want.

 **Listen to and read the excerpt. Then discuss the questions that follow.**

Give me your tired, your poor,
Your huddled masses[2] yearning[3] to breathe free,
The wretched[4] refuse[5] of your teeming[6] shore.
Send these, the homeless, tempest-tost[7] to me,
I lift my lamp beside the golden door!

(continued on next page)

[1] ***exiles:*** people forced to leave their countries
[2] ***huddled masses:*** groups of people pressed closely to each other
[3] ***yearn:*** to want greatly
[4] ***wretched:*** miserable; poor and extremely unhappy
[5] ***refuse:*** something thrown away as worthless
[6] ***teem:*** to crowd; to overfill
[7] ***tempest-tost:*** tossed or thrown in a storm

(a) Do you believe that the United States has lived up to the ideals in the poem? If so, how? If not, why not?

(b) Do you believe it is possible to live up to the ideals in the poem? Why or why not?

2. If you are an immigrant, why did you immigrate? What has your experience as an immigrant been like? If you are not an immigrant, would you consider immigrating? If so, under what circumstances?

3. Consider your native country or a country you know well. Do many people immigrate there? Where do the immigrants typically come from? Has immigration had any effects on the country? If so, what are they?

4. Consider your native country or a country you know well. Do many people emigrate from there? Where do the emigrants typically go? Has emigration had any effects on the country? If so, what are they?

ACTIVITY 2 PREPARING FOR THE LECTURE

The title of the lecture is "Immigration to the United States." What do you expect the lecturer to tell you in the lecture? Brainstorm ideas with your classmates.

Listen to the introduction. Check (✓) what the lecturer plans to do in the remainder of the lecture. (Check one or more.)

____ **a.** talk more about Native Americans or American Indians

____ **b.** talk more about whether the United States is a "melting pot" or a "stew"

____ **c.** talk about trends in U.S. immigration over the past 200 years or so

____ **d.** talk about immigration in 2005 in particular

ACTIVITY 3 LISTENING AND NOTING

You will hear a lecture about immigration from 1820 to 2004 and for 2005. Complete the chart on the next page with the correct numbers and information.

U.S. — land of immigrants

Only — true Americans

U.S. — melting pot? or stew?

IMMIGRATION	1820–2004		2005	
LOCATIONS	TOTAL #	%	TOTAL #	%
From all countries				
From continents				
Europe				
Asia				
Americas				
Africa				
Oceania				
From individual countries (country of birth)				
Mexico				
India				
China (mainland)				
Philippines				
Cuba				
Vietnam				
Dominican Republic				
Korea				
Colombia				
Ukraine				

ACTIVITY 4 REPLAY QUESTION

In discussions about immigration, what is the difference between viewing the United States as a "melting pot" and as a "stew"? Listen to the section from the lecture again and write the two different meanings.

1. "melting pot" view ______________________________

2. "stew" view ______________________________

LISTENING AND NOTE-TAKING STRATEGY

While you take notes, put a question mark next to numbers or facts that you're unsure about. After the lecture, ask classmates for those specific pieces of information: "Did you get how many people immigrated from Mexico in 2005?" Or ask your teacher at an appropriate time.

ACTIVITY 5 "OTHER VOICES" FOLLOW-UP

Students interviewed Americans to find out about their immigrant ancestors. Listen to two interviews and fill in the chart with the information you hear.

	Who did the speaker talk about?	When did the speaker's ancestor immigrate?	Where did the speaker's ancestor emigrate from?	Why did the speaker's ancestor immigrate?	What happened when the speaker's ancestor immigrated?
Interview #1	maternal grandfather				
	maternal grandmother				
Interview #2					

Listen to the third interview. The speaker says his brother paid a genealogist[1] to find out about his family's history, but he stopped. Why?

____

Is he telling the complete truth? ______________________________

[1] *genealogist:* a person who researches family history (names and details)

ACTIVITY 6 USING YOUR NOTES

1. Which pie chart best shows the breakdown of immigration by continent from 1820 to 2004?

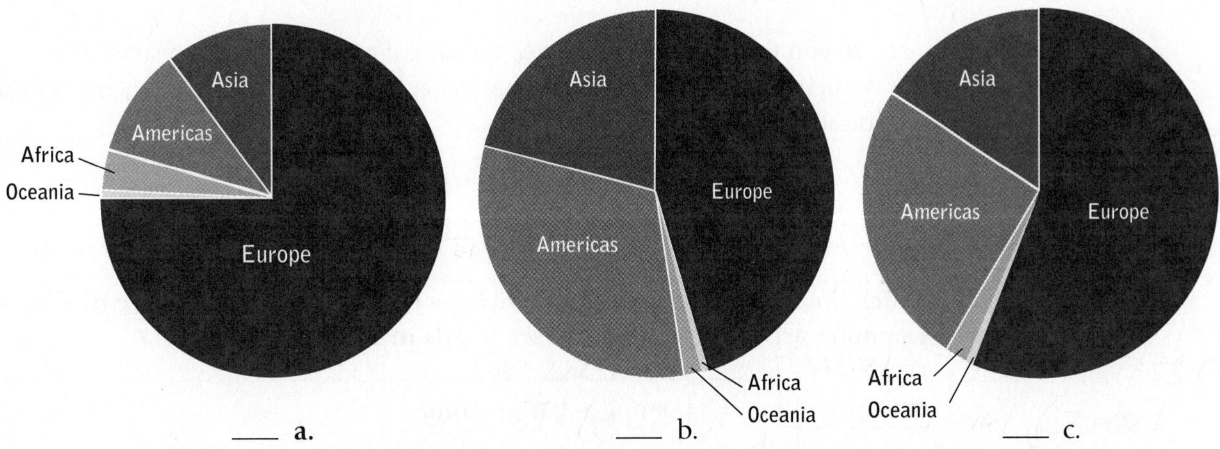

2. Draw a pie chart showing the breakdown of immigration by continent in 2005.

3. You will hear twelve statements about immigration statistics. Listen to each statement. Use your notes to decide whether each statement is true or false. Write *T* or *F*.

a. ___	d. ___	g. ___	j. ___
b. ___	e. ___	h. ___	k. ___
c. ___	f. ___	i. ___	l. ___

4. On a separate sheet of paper, write five statements about the immigration statistics that you just heard. Include both true and false statements.

   Test your classmates by reading your statements aloud and having them decide whether the statement is true or false, referring back to notes when necessary. If you disagree about any answers, listen to the lecture section again or ask for clarification.

Did you know?

From 1892 to 1954, nearly 12 million people passed through Ellis Island to immigrate to the United States. It is now a museum in New York harbor.

ACTIVITY 7 POST-LECTURE DISCUSSION

Discuss the following questions in small groups.

1. What did you find out from these statistics that you didn't know or expect?
2. Do you think the United States is more of a melting pot or a stew? Why? Which do you think it should be? What are the advantages of each one? the disadvantages?

ACTIVITY 8 ACADEMIC WORD LIST VOCABULARY

Match the word to its meaning. Write the correct letter in the space provided. Examples are given to help you see words in context.

Group 1

a. happening at a future time
b. relating to group characteristics (e.g., race, religion)
c. varied; different from each other
d. relating to areas

___	1. *diverse*	The students in this class come from diverse backgrounds.
___	2. *eventual*	Doctors told her to expect the eventual loss of her hearing.
___	3. *ethnic*	Different ethnic groups have different traditions.
___	4. *regional*	Can you hear regional language variations in the United States (e.g., the difference between speakers from New York and Boston)?

Group 2

a. a general pattern or direction
b. a change (to meet new conditions)
c. who or what someone is; a sense of self
d. an issue to be considered

___	5. *factor*	Salary wasn't the only factor she thought about when considering the job offer; she was also concerned about promotion possibilities.
___	6. *trend*	We're seeing a trend toward smaller families.
___	7. *identity*	He hid his identity by changing his voice and appearance.
___	8. *adjustment*	The technician made a small adjustment to the computer monitor and now everything is very clear.

Group 3

a. the larger percentage of the whole
b. what makes someone unique or special
c. object of attention
d. the people and places that make up a town or neighborhood

____ 9. *majority* The majority of people support the president.

____ 10. *individuality* He wears unusual clothing to express his individuality.

____ 11. *focus* He changed the focus of the study from illegal to legal immigration.

____ 12. *community* They didn't want to move because they loved the community they lived in.

ACTIVITY 9 USING VOCABULARY

Before reading, listen to a story that was originally told by the descendant of an immigrant. After listening, fill in the blanks with the vocabulary in the box. (You may change the verb forms and tenses. Not all words will be used.)

immigrate	*emigrate*	*ancestors*
melting pot	*descendants*	*retain*
blend in	*ethnic diversity*	

My ____________ (1.) came from Eastern Europe, primarily Poland and the former Soviet Union. Some ____________ (2.) to the United States for opportunities and adventures; others ____________ (3.) from their homeland because of persecution. They came to New York hoping that the city's great ____________ (4.) would allow them to ____________ (5.) with the crowds without being too noticeable. However, New York, the supposed ____________ (6.) of cultures, was in reality a stew. The new immigrants mixed with others but definitely ____________ (7.) their ethnic identity. I don't think they ever completely adjusted to their new lives.

VOCABULARY LEARNING STRATEGY

Active vocabulary learners are always looking for new words to learn. They consciously rehearse and practice words.

ACTIVITY 10 RETAINING VOCABULARY

Write on a separate sheet of paper at least five words from the lecture, poem, or discussion that you would like to remember. Use each word in two examples that will remind you of its meaning.

Example
identity: Because he was in the country illegally, he hid his true identity.

It was a case of mistaken identity and he wrongly went to prison.

ACTIVITY 11 BEYOND THE LECTURE: SPEAKING AND LISTENING

1. Research recent immigration to and emigration from your native country (or a country of your choice). Present your findings to your classmates using pie charts for visual support. Speculate about some reasons for and effects of that immigration.

2. Interview three native-born Americans about their family's immigration history. Create a chart like the example below. Share your findings with classmates.

Name	Who immigrated?	When did their ancestor immigrate? from where?	Why did their ancestor immigrate?	What did their ancestor do when he or she first arrived in the U.S.?	What happened over time?
Sergio Dominguez	mother	1970s, Venezuela	Education	Studied at university	Finished B.A. in biology. Homemaker.
	father	1970s, Mexico	Education	Studied at university	Got Ph.D. in chemistry. Worked in lab.

LISTENING FOR ORGANIZATION

(PART 1)

Goals

- Understand the importance of recognizing lecture organization plans
- Follow three organizational plans used by lecturers: defining a term, listing subtopics, exemplifying a topic
- Understand and follow the cues that signal these organizational plans
- Listen to and take notes on lectures using these organizational plans
- Practice using notes to answer various test-type questions

Discussion

Organization

1. Talk about the most organized people you know. In what ways are they organized? Is being organized a good quality in their cases?
2. How organized are you on a scale from 1 to 6 (1 = *very disorganized;* 6 = *very organized*)? How do you organize different things: space in your home, digital information, school supplies, materials, and information? Explain your ratings.
3. Different people can have very different styles of organization. Compare your organizing styles with your classmates' styles.
4. What is the value of "being organized"? What are some disadvantages of being disorganized? Are there any advantages to being disorganized?

Understanding the Importance of Recognizing Lecture Organization

When listening to a lecture, it's useful to figure out the lecturer's goals. For example, a lecturer might want the audience to

- learn a new or extended definition
- visualize something
- understand how something works
- understand the causes and consequences of a historical event

In almost all cases, lecturers organize their ideas in some way so that they can be more easily communicated. Some lecturers follow a strict outline, while others seem to talk more loosely. However, even those who seem to be talking extemporaneously are actually following some kind of organizational plan.

Research has shown that it is easier to remember information that is connected to a topic, a goal, or other information. Therefore, by recognizing the organization of a lecture, the listener can relate facts to each other and more easily

- understand the lecturer's goals
- predict the lecture's path and its conclusions
- remember information

Recognizing Organizational Plans within Lectures

Remember Rule 7 of the Dos and Don'ts for improving comprehension and note-taking:

> DON'T lose sight of the forest for the trees. (Don't listen for details before getting the larger picture.)
> DO listen for the lecturer's main points and for the general organizational framework.

Lectures can be organized on many levels. For example, the purpose of the *whole* lecture may be to show the cause-and-effect relationship between two events or to describe a process.

Within the lecture, there is also organization. For example, the lecturer's main goal may be to make a generalization and support it. However, to do that, the lecturer may define terms, provide examples, or describe processes.

Consider this example: A lecturer states, "There has been much research on the effects of alcohol on the development of the fetus" and then describes the research done on this from 1980 to the present. This lecturer is using two organizational plans: (1) making a generalization and providing evidence and (2) describing a sequence of events.

How does a listener recognize these organizational plans? Three plans are examined in more detail in this unit:

- Defining a term
- Listing subtopics
- Exemplifying (giving examples)

Other plans will be examined in later chapters.

Defining Terms through Simple and Extended Definitions

Lecturers can define a term in two ways. A *simple definition* is a single statement, such as "An accomplice is a legal term referring to an individual who joins with another individual to complete a crime." An *extended definition* gives more detail, and can include examples, analogies, or other supporting information. An extended definition might even be a whole lecture!

Notes from a lecture using this pattern might look like this:

> Accomplice (legal term): individual who joins w/ another indiv to commit crime
>
> — has = responsibility under law

When the lecturer gives a definition, the listener's task is to note the key words or the ideas that make up the definition.

CUES TO RECOGNIZE SIMPLE AND EXTENDED DEFINITIONS

1. Rhetorical questions referring back to a term requiring a definition or explanation:

   What is meant by X?

   How can we best define X?

   What is a definition of X that we can work with?

   Can anyone give me a definition of X?

2. Words or phrases signaling a definition or explanation:

   (Now) X means more than just… it also means…

   By X, I (mean / meant / referred to) …

   When I used X, I (meant / was referring to) …

   That is to say,

   In other words, …

   To put it another way, …

   Or …, to use another term.

3. Terms written on the board and explained:

Accomplice:

4. Terms followed by appositives (noun phrase definitions):

They are accomplices … conspirators in crime …

5. Stress, intonation, and pauses used with appositives:

They are accomplices … conspirators in crime …

Note the strong stress on the words *accomplices* and *conspirators* and the secondary stress on *crime*, which emphasize their importance. Note the pause between *accomplices* and *conspirators*. Finally, note the repetition of the stress pattern for *accomplices* and *conspirators*. These paralinguistic features (stress, intonation, pauses) all carry meaning.

Exercise 1

Listen for the appositive in each of the following excerpts. Write the meaning of each word.

Example

entities: things

1. hearth cooking centre small area in the... yard
2. episodic memory specific events ; type of memory
3. antecedent things came first to make motion pictures
4. affect emotional approach, behaviour possible (taking action)

   cognition thought, mind

Exercise 2

Listen to each of the following lecture excerpts and write the definitions on a separate sheet of paper.

Example

In this excerpt from a lecture on the costs or benefits of employment to women, the lecturer defines the term *emotional strength*.

emotional strength: the degree of psych. distress to which s.o. reacts to life crisis

1. In this excerpt from an anthropology lecture, the lecturer defines two contrasting terms: *paleontology* and *paleoanthropology*.
2. In this excerpt from a lecture on ecology, the lecturer gives the term *metabolism* and follows it with a definition.
3. In this excerpt from a lecture on ecology, the lecturer names the term *irritability* and follows it with a definition.
4. In this excerpt from a lecture on ecology, the lecturer defines *life* by giving the criteria for judging life. The lecturer ends by tying the information together into a simple definition.

D Listing Subtopics

Here, the lecturer breaks a topic down by listing or enumerating a number of features of the topic. For example, in this medical lecture about autism, the lecturer says that autism is defined on the basis of behavior, and she lists those behaviors.

Notes from this lecture might look like this:

Heading	Autism: disease affecting 1 in 100 children/adults Diagnosed on basis of behavior
List	–social impairment –communication impairment –rigid & restricted behavior and interests

Each item in the list is related to the larger heading in the same way; that is, they are all behaviors associated with autism. They are all indented an equal amount under the heading.

CUES TO RECOGNIZE LISTS

1. Numbers indicating listed items:

   The first (second, etc.) point is ...
   Number one (two, etc.) ...
   First (second, etc.) of all ...

2. Stress emphasizing numbers:

   The first stage of the process is ...
   The focus of my talk is on two main areas, X and Y.
   A second type of cell is called...
   The third important thing to remember about this time period is...

3. Phrases or sentences signaling a list of forthcoming items:

   There are three people who have influenced her work.
   Let me start with the five goals of the organization.
   Stendhal's influence on the modern French novel can be seen in a number of ways.

You will hear three lecture excerpts that list information. First read the information about each excerpt. Then listen and take notes in the spaces provided.

Example
Excerpt from a lecture on psychology

VOCABULARY

agenda: a list, plan, or outline of what needs to be done

	Seligman: President of APA (American Psych. Assoc.) 1996
Heading	Agenda:
List	1. to make psychology more applied
	2. to start POSITIVE psychology

1. Excerpt from a lecture on market research

Heading	Research: what do people carry? (Why? People pay for important stuff!)
List	Most important
	1. Keys
	2. Money
	3. Phone

2. Excerpt from a lecture on human development.

VOCABULARY

premature: occurring before the expected time
fetus: an unborn being (in humans, from the ninth week to birth)
womb: the place in the mother's body where the fetus develops
incubator: a machine providing an ideal environment for the development of premature babies
monitor: to watch carefully; to check regularly
kid: (informal) a child

Heading: What needs to be done to keep premature kid alive?

List:
1. constent monitoring of oxigen levels   breathing by its on
2. mentain kid's temperature at the appropriate level   hot so high
keep things warm   ↑blindness!
keep things warm

3. Excerpt from a lecture on human development.

VOCABULARY

fetal: relating to the fetus
embryo: an organism in the earliest stages of development, before it becomes a fetus
cell: the smallest unit of an organism that can function independently

Heading: 3 things that happen during prenatal period

List:
1. frauth become grater   ① Multiplying/devide/proliferation
2. Change their properties   ② Differentiate
3. Movement of the cells

Exemplifying a Topic

A lecturer can clarify the topic by giving examples. In this lecture about art, the speaker gives examples of what a viewer might want to look at when considering a piece of art.

Notes from a lecture using this pattern might look like this:

Heading	Observe physical properties of artwork
Examples	e.g. size?
	medium?[1]
	How medium applied?
	Texture?
	2D or 3D?

CUES TO RECOGNIZE EXAMPLES

1. Phrases signaling an example:
   For example/For instance, ...
   To illustrate this, ...
   One example of this would be...
   Let's say, ...
   Take something like this ...
   A typical case would be...

2. Phrases or sentences emphasizing the application of a concept:
   Let me give an example of how this works.
   In order to understand this more clearly, ...
   In more concrete terms, ...
   Let's take a look at a practical application of this theory.
   Here's one major benefit of this technique:

3. Rhetorical questions signaling an example:
   Now, where can we find an example of this?
   What does this look like in the real world?

[1] ***medium:*** the material or technique with which an artist works (e.g., watercolor, oil)

Exercise 4

You will hear three lecture excerpts that include examples. First read the information about each excerpt. Then, while listening to the excerpt, take notes in the spaces provided.

Example

Excerpt from a lecture on ecology.

Heading	Level of light that plants tolerate varies greatly
Examples	e.g., shade plants — need low light; die in sun
	other plants — sit in sun all day
	not just temp. — also light intensity

1. Excerpt from a lecture on eight steps of topic analysis for library research.

Heading	2nd step — Break topic into subtopics
Examples	e.g.,

2. Excerpt from a lecture on family systems.

VOCABULARY

boundary: something that indicates a limit

caste system: a social system that divides society into groups that are restricted in terms of occupation and marriage

Heading	Endogamy sometimes in marriage patterns
Definition	
Examples	e.g.,

3. Excerpt from a lecture on memory.

Heading + definition	Episodic: memories of specific events in life
Examples	e.g.
Heading + definition	Semantic mems: general knowledge
Examples	e.g.

LECTURE 5

Amnesty International (Political Science/ Management)

Vocabulary

Related to Human Rights

Check (✓) the words you know. Underline the words you want to learn. Then check their meaning with your instructor or in a dictionary.

freedom of speech
freedom of press
freedom of assembly
freedom of association

human rights
civil liberties

human rights violations/abuses

to oppress/oppression
to persecute/persecution
to torture
to deprive of freedom
to hold in custody
to detain/detention

to execute/execution
death penalty

detainee
prisoner

to censor/censorship

to dissent/dissenter

amnesty

ACTIVITY 1 **PRE-LECTURE DISCUSSION**

Discuss the following in small groups.

1. Each of the following drawings attempts to communicate ideas and feelings. Discuss what you believe the artists were attempting to communicate, and which is most effective.

a. 

Drawing given to Amnesty International by Pablo Picasso

b. 

The Amnesty International logo

c. 

Graphic from an Amnesty International publication

2. Judging from thes graphics can you guess what Amnesty International does? What do you already know about Amnesty International? What does "human rights" mean to you?

ACTIVITY 2 PREPARING FOR THE LECTURE

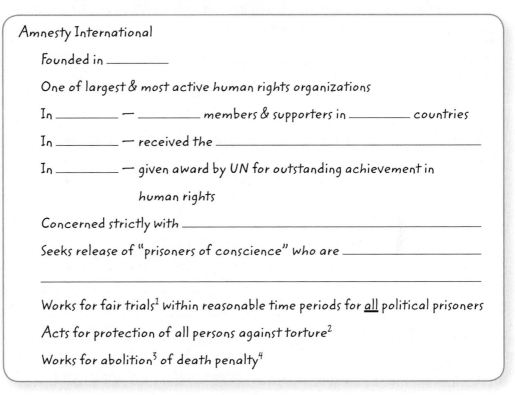

The lecture's introduction tells you what Amnesty International does. First review the vocabulary in this exercise. Then listen to the introduction and fill in the blanks with the missing dates, statistics, and other information.

Amnesty International

Founded in ________

One of largest & most active human rights organizations

In ________ — ________ members & supporters in ________ countries

In ________ — received the ________________________

In ________ — given award by UN for outstanding achievement in human rights

Concerned strictly with ________________________

Seeks release of "prisoners of conscience" who are ________________________

____

Works for fair trials[1] within reasonable time periods for all political prisoners

Acts for protection of all persons against torture[2]

Works for abolition[3] of death penalty[4]

The introduction ends with the following words:

> *Okay… what I'm specifically going to focus on in this lecture ... now that I've told you a little bit about the organization ... are some of the specific principles that underlie some of Amnesty International's activities … and probably contribute to its success … okay … and there are eight principles in particular that I'm going to talk about … and then before I end, I'm going to give you a specific example of an individual whose life was probably saved by Amnesty International's work just so you can get an idea of the organization's work in practice … but let's start … as I said … with the principles …*

What do you expect the lecturer to say in the remainder of the lecture?

---

1 ***trial:*** a legal procedure before a judge to establish facts and decide guilt or innocence

2 ***torture:*** abusive treatment causing great emotional and physical pain

3 ***abolish:*** to bring a law or condition to an end

4 ***death penalty:*** execution as a result of conviction of a crime

ACTIVITY 3 LISTENING FOR THE LARGER PICTURE

Listen to the complete lecture. Note the eight principles underlying Amnesty International's activities and success. You will hear several details for each of these principles. At this time, note only the principles. In addition, listen to the story of Luiz Rossi. Don't worry about the details of his story; just focus on the general events.

VOCABULARY

mandate: a right or order to act according to members' wishes
impartiality: the state of not taking sides or being biased

Eight Principles Underlying Amnesty International's Activities and Success

1. ______
2. ______
3. ______
4. ______
5. ______
6. ______
7. ______
8. ______

Compare your list of principles to a classmate's list.

Discuss what happened to Luiz Rossi. What do you remember about the events?

ACTIVITY 4 ORGANIZATION

Read this summary of the lecture organization.

The primary organizational plan of this lecture is to break down a topic by *listing* its features. The lecture lists the eight principles underlying Amnesty International's work. The lecturer also gives an extended *example* of the organization's work in practice. In addition, he defines a few terms such as "prisoner of conscience" and "adoption group."

What do you remember about each principle? Discuss with a partner.

ACTIVITY 5 DEFINING VOCABULARY

The following words and expressions were used in the lecture. You may remember the contexts in which you heard them. Listen to another example of each word or expression in a new context. Check (✓) the letter of the definition that most closely matches what you think the word or expression means.

1. ***on behalf* of someone***

   ___ **a.** against the interests of someone

   ___ **b.** representing only a small part of someone's interests

   ___ **c.** in the interests of someone or for someone

2. ***appeal***

   ___ **a.** a very strong request (for help, assistance)

   ___ **b.** a sweet, crispy fruit, typically red or green

   ___ **c.** angry, harsh words, spoken in a loud voice

3. ***credibility***

   ___ **a.** the quality of being trustworthy

   ___ **b.** the quality of being unbelievable

   ___ **c.** the ability to get financial resources

4. ***economic sanctions***

   ___ **a.** economic assistance given to support a country whose citizens are suffering

   ___ **b.** economic actions taken against a country that has broken a law or rule

   ___ **c.** economic research that is designed to avoid heavy taxes or high prices

5. ***persuasion***

   ___ **a.** the ability to influence others through reasoning

   ___ **b.** the necessity of punishing children when they behave poorly

   ___ **c.** the typical physical and emotional development from childhood to adulthood

6. ***pursue****

   ___ **a.** to spend money on; to finance

   ___ **b.** to avoid or delay

   ___ **c.** to continue steadily with

(continued on next page)

7. *found**

___ a. to locate something lost

___ b. to establish or set up

___ c. to teach or educate

8. *sole**

___ a. only; single

___ b. poorest

___ c. relating to the spirit

9. *with no strings attached*

___ a. not containing any mechanical or electrical parts that can break easily

___ b. not needing a lot of care to maintain

___ c. with no limiting conditions (on something agreed upon or received)

10. *urgent*

___ a. requiring great financial expense

___ b. demanding immediate attention

___ c. fulfilling a personal need

11. *campaign*

___ a. a bubbly alcoholic drink

___ b. a series of energetic actions taken to reach a goal

___ c. an outdoor activity offering experience in nature

12. *network**

___ a. a system of connections

___ b. an item made of string or wire that is twisted together

___ c. an activity that takes place on the Internet

ACTIVITY 6 LISTENING AND NOTE-TAKING

Listen to the lecture a second time. Take notes using the following format, but use your own paper and allow more space.

Introduction	
List: principles underlying AI's work	Principles Underlying AI's Activities & Success:
Principle 1	1.
Principle 2	2.
Principle 3	3.
Principle 4	4.
Principle 5	5.
Principle 6	6.
Principle 7	7.
Principle 8	8.
Example	Urgent Action Network: example of 1st campaign: Luiz Rossi
Conclusions	

ACTIVITY 7 REPLAY QUESTION

"In order to" signals an action/result or cause/effect relationship. Consider the following: "Stop smoking in order to get healthy," or "In order to get healthy, stop smoking." What is the desired result? What is the necessary action? (Note that "in order to" can be reduced to an infinitive form with the same meaning: "To get healthy, stop smoking.")

Listen to five excerpts from the lecture and note the desired result.

1. Desired result: ______________________________

   Necessary action: It's necessary to have reliable information.

2. Desired result: ______________________________

   Necessary action: You need to have reliable information.

(continued on next page)

3. Desired result: ______________________________

   Necessary action: They conduct fact-finding missions.

4. Desired result: ______________________________

   Necessary action: They refuse to compare or rank countries.

5. Desired result: ______________________________

   Necessary action: There are certain rules that Amnesty International has adopted.

LISTENING AND NOTE-TAKING STRATEGIES

1. Review your notes as soon as possible after listening. Perhaps there was information that you heard but had no time to note. Add information that you remember.
2. Ask classmates for specific pieces of information that you might have missed: "I didn't catch the seventh principle. Did you get that?"
3. Rewrite your notes soon after listening. Make the relationship between ideas clear and make important ideas stand out by, for example, indenting or using headings.

ACTIVITY 8 "OTHER VOICES" FOLLOW-UP

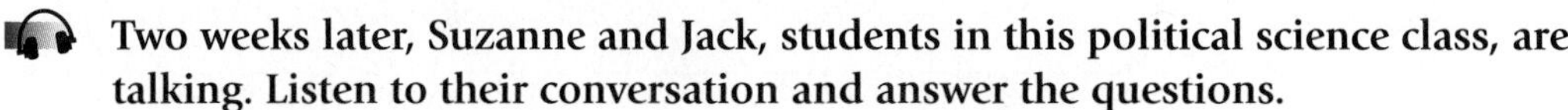

Two weeks later, Suzanne and Jack, students in this political science class, are talking. Listen to their conversation and answer the questions.

1. Check (✓) the answer: Suzanne, Jack, or both.

	SUZANNE	JACK
a. Who became interested in doing something about human rights after the lecture?		
b. Who had already looked at Amnesty International's Web site?		
c. Who had already gone to an Amnesty International meeting?		
d. Who works in addition to going to school?		
e. Who had the wrong information about Eritrea?		
f. Who is definitely going to the next Amnesty International meeting?		

2. What is true about the Amnesty International group that was mentioned in the conversation? Check (✓) one or more answers.

___ a. They meet weekly.

___ b. They meet on Tuesdays at 4:00.

___ c. They are planning a campus event related to human rights.

___ d. They are particularly interested in human rights issues related to women and children.

___ e. They are particularly interested in the relationship between corporations and human rights.

___ f. One of the members of that group is a former prisoner of conscience in Eritrea.

___ g. They wrote letters to government officials at the last meeting.

___ h. About a dozen people attended the meeting.

___ i. They want to bring a former prisoner of conscience to the campus to speak.

___ j. There was food at the end of the meeting.

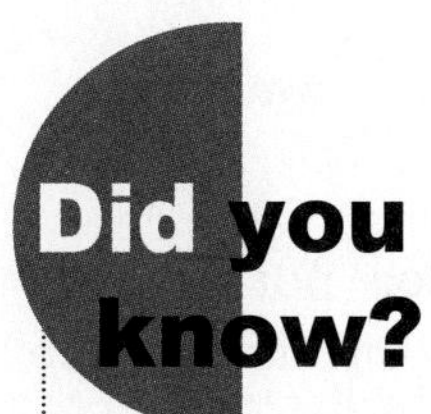

Actor and filmmaker Nicolas Cage donated $2 million to Amnesty International to establish a fund to help former child soldiers.

3. Which of the following is NOT true about Suzanne?

___ a. She would like Jack to come to the next meeting.

___ b. She thinks Jack has lots of available time that he wastes.

___ c. She is enthusiastic about the campus Amnesty International group.

___ d. She expects Jack to come to the next meeting.

ACTIVITY 9 POST-LECTURE READING AND DISCUSSION

Discuss the following in small groups.

1. Do you think Amnesty International serves an important purpose? Why or why not?
2. Read the following poem. What does this poem mean to you?

They came for the Communists, and I
didn't object—For I wasn't a Communist;
They came for the Socialists, and I
didn't object—For I wasn't a Socialist;
They came for the labor leaders, and I
didn't object—For I wasn't a labor leader;
They came for the Jews, and I
didn't object—For I wasn't a Jew;
Then they came for me—
And there was no one left to object.

—***Martin Niemoller,*** German Protestant pastor (1892–1984)

ACTIVITY 10 USING YOUR NOTES

Use your notes to answer the following questions. Write your answers for 3, 4, and 5 on a separate sheet of paper.

1. Infer whether each statement is true or false. The lecturer does not explicitly make these statements, but a thoughtful listener can draw conclusions from the lecture. Write *T* or *F*. Be prepared to support your answers.

   ___ **a.** AI is an organization that works predominantly in the abstract sense (i.e., it focuses on large-scale, intangible, immaterial goals).

   ___ **b.** AI feels that punishment of countries with a bad human rights record is necessary.

   ___ **c.** AI is basically a Western organization and is somewhat anti-Communist.

   ___ **d.** AI publishes a "Ten Worst Countries for Human Rights" list every year.

2. Which of the following statements is Amnesty International likely to support? Check (✓) as many as are applicable. Be prepared to support your answers.

   ___ **a.** It is better to focus on a limited area than to cover all the wrongs in the world.

   ___ **b.** The strength of a group rests with its individual members.

   ___ **c.** Change is brought about through military or economic pressure on a government.

   ___ **d.** Taking swift action is more important than getting all the facts.

   ___ **e.** It is important to set priorities, decide which countries are the worst in terms of human rights, and work there.

   ___ **f.** We are all citizens of the world when it comes to involvement with human rights.

   ___ **g.** Let's talk specifics, not abstractions.

   ___ **h.** In order to change the world, you must start with yourself.

   ___ **i.** If you are not part of the solution, you're part of the problem.

3. What is an Amnesty International adoption group?

4. How does Amnesty International ensure its impartiality? State at least two ways.

5. In what year did the Urgent Action Network begin? What is the story behind the first Urgent Action Network letter-writing campaign?

ACTIVITY 11 COMPARING IDEAS

1. Compare your answers to the preceding questions. If you have different answers, check your notes and discuss your reasons for making your choices.

2. Compare your rewritten notes to the sample rewritten notes in Appendix D. Notice the organization. Is yours similar or different? Are your notes equally effective in making important ideas stand out?

ACTIVITY 12 ACADEMIC WORD LIST VOCABULARY

1. Do you know the meanings of the words in this chart? If not, ask a classmate or look up the word. Then fill in the chart with the noun forms.

VERB	NOUN
isolate	
violate	
investigate	
justify	
participate	

VERB	NOUN
expand	
consult	
survive	
require	
acknowledge	

2. Choose one of the words above to complete the following sentences. The meaning of the word you need is in parentheses. You may change verb forms.

   a. The police are (researching) ________________ the fire's causes.

   b. Our business (growth) ________________ is going well; soon we'll have branches in five cities.

   c. The prisoner wasn't sure that she would (remain alive) ________________ to tell her story.

   d. We require each person's (involvement in a group action) ________________ in order to make this project work.

   e. There is no (explanatory reason) ________________ for her behavior.

   f. You have no choice; this is a (necessity) ________________.

   g. You should (seek advice from) ________________ a doctor.

   h. With new friends, he no longer has a sense of (aloneness) ________________.

   i. I can't forgive her for lying to me; she (broke a law / rule / contract) ________________ my trust.

   j. It took two weeks for the police to (admit the truth of) ________________ Professor Rossi's detention.

ACTIVITY 13 USING VOCABULARY

You will hear vocabulary from this lecture in different contexts. Check (✓) the letter of the closest paraphrase of the information that you heard.

1. ___ **a.** The police held him, but no one hurt him.
   ___ **b.** The police held him, but no one helped him.
   ___ **c.** The police helped him, but no one else would.

2. ___ **a.** Everyone except Mary voted for the new law.
   ___ **b.** Mary was the only one who voted.
   ___ **c.** Mary voted in the same manner as everyone else did.

3. ___ **a.** People in many parts of the world want the death penalty.
   ___ **b.** People in many parts of the world are working to establish the death penalty.
   ___ **c.** People in many parts of the world want to get rid of the death penalty.

4. ___ **a.** People stopped trusting the judge because she favored one side over another.
   ___ **b.** People began to trust the judge because she was fair to all sides.
   ___ **c.** The judge lost her job because people thought she was untruthful.

5. ___ **a.** He was honored because he prevented human rights abuses.
   ___ **b.** He was detained because he permitted human rights abuses.
   ___ **c.** He was executed because he permitted human rights abuses.

6. ___ **a.** They tried to persuade the governor to kill the criminal.
   ___ **b.** They tried to persuade the governor not to kill the criminal.
   ___ **c.** Their defense of the criminal made the governor angry.

7. ___ **a.** Someone gave money to the organization and expected nothing in return.
   ___ **b.** Someone gave money to the organization but expected something in return.
   ___ **c.** Someone questioned an unusual package that was sent to the organization.

8. ___ **a.** Her father convinced her to give up her goals.
   ___ **b.** Her father showed her how unrealistic her goals were.
   ___ **c.** Her father convinced her to keep working toward her goals.

ACTIVITY 14 RETAINING VOCABULARY

VOCABULARY LEARNING STRATEGY

Create flashcards to help you remember new words and their definitions. Review them regularly. On the front of the card, write the word. (If you found the word in a complete sentence, it is helpful to copy that sentence too.) On the back of the card, write the definition or draw a picture that defines the word.

Choose ten words from the lecture, poem, or discussion that you would like to remember. Then create flashcards. Exchange your flashcards with a partner and quiz each other.

ACTIVITY 15 BEYOND THE LECTURE: SPEAKING AND LISTENING

A debate is an organized discussion involving two opposing views. Good debaters present support for their own side and also counter arguments from their opponents.

As a class, choose one of the following debate topics:

1. Internal Affairs and International Relations

   Team A: Human rights abuses are international issues that should be of concern to foreign governments, trade partners, and others in the international community.

   Team B: Human rights abuses are issues that should be handled internally without international interference.

OR

2. Amnesty International's Principles

   Team A: Amnesty International's principles are the best means by which to deal with the problems of human rights violations.

   Team B: Amnesty International's principles need changing. There are more effective ways to deal with human rights violations.

Students should form two groups: Team A and Team B. Each team meets to discuss arguments to support its position and ways to respond to the other team's counterarguments. At the end of their discussion, each team selects three team members to represent them in the debate.

(continued on next page)

On each team, one member is responsible for presenting the major arguments for the group's position. A second member is responsible for providing the counterargument. The third member is responsible for providing a final wrap-up and argument. Class members who are not speaking in the debate are responsible for noting the key points that each team makes.

The debate takes place in the following order:

1. Flip a coin to decide which team goes first.
2. The first team presents arguments to support its position. (5 minute maximum)
3. The second team presents arguments to support its position. (5 minute maximum)
4. The first team counters the second team's arguments. (3 minute maximum)
5. The second team counters the first team's arguments. (3 minute maximum)
6. The first team wraps up. (2 minute maximum)
7. The second team wraps up. (2 minute maximum)
8. At the end of the debate, the teacher decides which team wins.

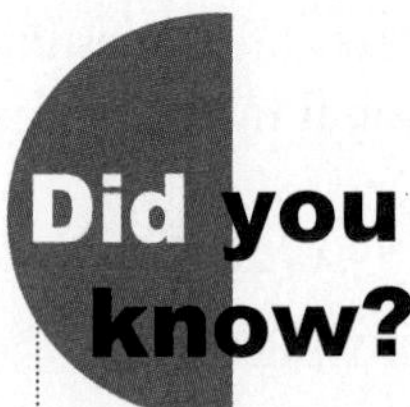

The U.N. General Assembly adopted the Universal Declaration of Human Rights on December 10, 1948. This document includes 30 specific areas of basic human rights. You can find it in English at http://www.un.org/en/documents/udhr/.

LECTURE 6

Two 21st Century Eco-Heroes (Ecology)

Vocabulary

Check (✓) the words you know. Underline the words you want to learn. Then check their meaning with your instructor or in a dictionary.

Related to Ecology
ecology
ecosystem
environment

environmentalist
ecologist

conservation
recycling

Related to Awards
honor/honoree
prize/prizewinner
award/award winner

grant (recipient)
scholarship (recipient)
fellowship (recipient)

to recognize
to nominate
to award

ACTIVITY 1 PRE-LECTURE DISCUSSION

Discuss the following in small groups.

1. What are the characteristics of a "hero"? Write 10 sentences starting with "A hero is someone who …."

2. The following are current ecological problems facing our world. Which would you rank as the three most important? Check (✓) them.

    ___ air and water pollution
    ___ global warming
    ___ deforestation (the destruction and loss of forests) and land erosion (the wearing down or loss of soil from the earth's surface)
    ___ destruction of animal habitats (living environments)
    ___ loss of animal and plant species
    ___ overconsumption of natural resources (such as oil, gas, wood)
    ___ overpopulation
    ___ urban (city) growth and the movement of great numbers of people from rural (countryside, farm) to urban environments
    ___ drought (periods of time with limited or no rain) and desertification (the change of healthy farmable land to deserts)
    ___ waste management (including radioactive waste)
    ___ other ____________________

Do you know of any "eco-heroes" who work in these areas?

ACTIVITY 2 PREPARING FOR THE LECTURE

 **Listen to the introduction of the lecture.**

VOCABULARY

will: a legal statement of the distribution of goods after one's death
mankind: humanity
preceding:* coming before
global:* relating to the world as a whole
benefit:* to be of service to; to do good for

1. The lecturer asks two different questions. What are they, and what are the answers?
2. What will the lecturer speak about in the remainder of the lecture?

ACTIVITY 3 LISTENING FOR THE LARGER PICTURE

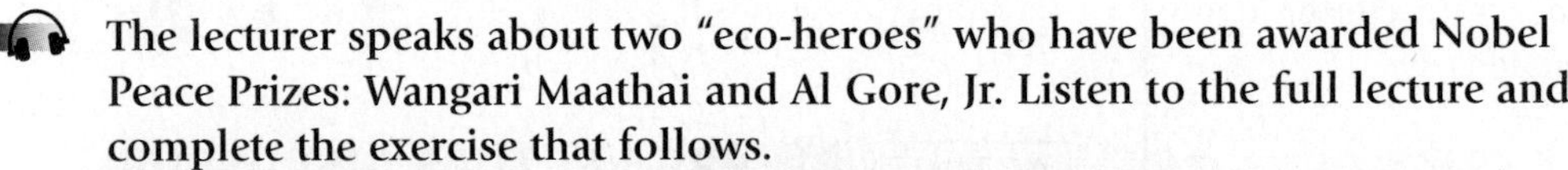

The lecturer speaks about two "eco-heroes" who have been awarded Nobel Peace Prizes: Wangari Maathai and Al Gore, Jr. Listen to the full lecture and complete the exercise that follows.

1. In the chart on the next page, check (✓) the appropriate box showing which topics the lecturer mentioned and who the lecturer spoke about. Don't write the specific information now.

	MAATHAI	GORE
Place of birth	✓	
Date of birth		
Family status (marriage, children)		
Professional training		
Imprisonment(s)		
Elected or appointed governmental position(s)		
Founded a movement called the "Green Belt Movement"		
Founded a political party		
Produced an Academy Award-winning movie		
Educated people about environmental problems		
Worked largely with poor women doing "grassroots" work		
Said, "It's time to make peace with our planet."		

ACTIVITY 4 ORGANIZATION

Read this summary of the lecture organization.

The organizational plan of this lecture is primarily *listing and exemplifying*. The lecturer lists two eco-heroes who have won the Nobel Peace Prize in the 21st century and gives examples of their activist and ecological work. In addition, the lecturer defines a few terms such as "global warming" and "desertification."

What do you remember about Maathai's life and work? Gore's? Discuss with a partner.

ACTIVITY 5 DEFINING VOCABULARY

The following words and expressions were used in the lecture. You may remember the contexts in which you heard them. Listen to another example of each word or expression in a new context. Check (✓) the letter of the definition that most closely matches what you think the word or expression means.

1. *shift*

   ____ a. change

   ____ b. support

   ____ c. hopefulness

(continued on next page)

2. *resign*

____ a. to extend one's job contract

____ b. to choose to leave one's job

____ c. to say something over and over again

3. *intention*

____ a. concentration or focus

____ b. aim or plan that guides one's actions

____ c. injury, typically occurring after an accident

4. *quote**

____ a. a word-for-word retelling of someone's words

____ b. a picture of a famous person

____ c. a famous political leader's historical importance

5. *impact**

____ a. entertainment value

____ b. financial value or worth

____ c. effect or influence

6. *restore**

____ a. to bring back to an original condition

____ b. to put something away for later use

____ c. to buy again

7. *poverty*

____ a. the state of being poor

____ b. the state of being frightened

____ c. the state of being powerful

8. *debate**

____ a. a steady decline in numbers or quality

____ b. an environmental solution to a difficult problem

____ c. a formal argument or discussion

9. *stray*

____ a. to destroy something old in order to bring in new ideas

____ b. to make clients or customers angry and uncomfortable

____ c. to leave one's original path and go outside expected boundaries

ACTIVITY 6 LISTENING AND NOTE-TAKING

Listen to the lecture a second time. Take notes using the following format, but use your own paper and allow more space.

Introduction: Facts about the Nobel Prize	*Nobel Prizes*
List of types	*Types:*
Details about founder	*Alfred Nobel:*
List of two people who've won the Nobel Peace Prize	*2 recent winners of Peace Prize (for work in ecology)* *Note shift in thinking: in past, peace = prevent war* *Now, incl. ecological work*
Details of Maathai's life & examples of her work	*Wangari Maathai*
Details of Al Gore, Jr.'s life & examples of his work	*Al Gore, Jr.*
Conclusions	

ACTIVITY 7 REPLAY QUESTIONS

Listen to each excerpt from the lecture and answer the questions.

1. According to the lecturer, Alfred Nobel defined "peace" in a "limited sense of preventing war or violence," but the Nobel Prize Award Committee has expanded that definition to include ecological work. How does the lecturer think they might justify this expanded definition?

   Add to the notes below with the reasons that the lecturer gives.

> 2 recent winners of Nobel <u>Peace</u> Prize (for work in <u>ecology</u>!)
>
> Note shift in thinking: in past, peace = prevent war
>
> Now incl. ecological work
>
> Justification? ______________________

2. Does the lecturer believe that Alfred Nobel intended his Peace Prize to include ecological work?

   a. ___ definitely yes

   b. ___ probably not

   c. ___ probably yes

   d. ___ definitely not

LISTENING AND NOTE-TAKING STRATEGIES

1. Review your notes as soon as possible after listening. Add information that you remember but didn't have time to note.
2. Ask classmates for specific pieces of information that you might have missed: "I missed a few things about Maathai's work in the 1980s. Do you have anything in your notes about that?"
3. Rewrite your notes soon after listening, if necessary. Add details and clarify relationships among ideas.

ACTIVITY 8 "OTHER VOICES" FOLLOW-UP

A student asks the professor about the environmental studies field after class. Listen to their conversation and answer the following questions.

1. The student asked the professor, "Is it too early for me to think about majoring in environmental science?" The professor

   ___ **a.** said "Yes, it is."

   ___ **b.** said "No, it isn't."

   ___ **c.** didn't answer this question.

2. The student asked the professor about the job prospects in the area of environmental science. The professor

   ___ **a.** said that prospects are good (i.e., that there are many jobs expected in the future).

   ___ **b.** said that prospects are bad (i.e., that there aren't many jobs expected in the future).

   ___ **c.** didn't answer this question.

3. The student asked how the professor got to her position in the field. The professor talked about

   ___ **a.** her degrees and specializations.

   ___ **b.** where she went to school.

   ___ **c.** how she became interested in the field.

4. What advice did the professor NOT give the student?

   ___ **a.** Take basic courses like "Intro to the Environment" or "Intro to Ecology."

   ___ **b.** Narrow your focus when you get a master's or Ph.D. degree.

   ___ **c.** Find out what you're most interested in.

   ___ **d.** Major in the professor's specialization, biodiversity.

5. Which sentence is probably true?

   ___ **a.** The professor is enthusiastic about the field.

   ___ **b.** The professor doesn't want to talk to this student.

   ___ **c.** The student is thinking about majoring in environmental science because he is worried about the environment.

   ___ **d.** The student doesn't feel that the professor answered his questions.

ACTIVITY 9 POST-LECTURE DISCUSSION

Discuss the following in small groups.

1. The lecturer quoted Al Gore, Jr. talking about global warming: "We, the human species, are confronting a planetary emergency—a threat to the survival of our civilization.... The scientists are virtually screaming from the rooftops now. The debate is over! There's no longer any debate in the scientific community about this. But the political systems around the world have held this at arm's length because it's an inconvenient truth."
   a. What do you know about global warming? What effects of global warming, if any, are you aware of?
   b. What does Gore mean when he says that the political systems have held this [the issue of global warming] at arm's length?
   c. Why does Gore believe that global warming is an "inconvenient truth"?
   d. According to Gore, are scientists and political leaders "on the same page" about the threat of global warming (that is, are they working together and seeing the issue similarly)?
   e. What is your reaction to Gore's quote?

Gandhi (20th century Indian pacifist) never received the Nobel Peace Prize, although he was nominated five times.

2. The lecturer ends with a question to consider: "The Nobel Prize Award Committee is clearly affirming a connection between peace and environmental work. So what do you think? Have they strayed too far from Alfred Nobel's more narrow understanding of a 'peace' prize ... or is this the type of peace that we need to be recognizing?" How would you answer this question?

ACTIVITY 10 USING YOUR NOTES

Use your notes to answer the following questions.

1. Which of the following is NOT true about Alfred Nobel?
   ___ a. He was a scientist, industrialist, and inventor.
   ___ b. He invented dynamite, a kind of explosive.
   ___ c. When he died, he left his fortune to his family.
   ___ d. He was born in Sweden in the 1800s.

2. Which of the following are Maathai's accomplishments and experiences, according to the lecture? Check (✓) one or more.

____ a. She was the first woman to receive the Nobel Peace Prize.

____ b. She was the first woman from Africa to receive the Nobel Peace Prize.

____ c. She was the first woman from Africa to receive a doctorate (i.e., Ph.D. degree.)

____ d. She became the first female professor at the University of Nairobi.

____ e. She has worked as a professor at the university for more than three decades.

____ f. She founded a movement to plant grass.

____ g. She founded a grassroots movement to plant trees.

____ h. She became a leader in the pro-democracy movement in the 1980s.

____ i. She was elected to Parliament.

____ j. She was appointed Minister of Health.

____ k. She founded the Kenyan Green Party.

3. The Green Belt Movement that Maathai founded has had numerous goals. List three of them.

a. ____________________

b. ____________________

c. ____________________

4. According to the lecturer, what is Al Gore, Jr. best known for worldwide?

____ a. his discovery of global warming

____ b. his persistence in educating people and demanding action about global warming

____ c. his acting in a movie called *An Inconvenient Truth*

____ d. his American political career as a state representative, vice-president, and presidential candidate

ACTIVITY 11 COMPARING IDEAS

1. Compare your answers to the preceding questions. If you have different answers, check your notes and discuss your reasons for making your choices.

2. Compare your rewritten notes to the sample rewritten notes in Appendix D. Notice the organization. Is yours similar or different? Are your notes equally effective in making important ideas stand out?

ACTIVITY 12 ACADEMIC WORD LIST PRACTICE

1. Do you know the meanings of the words in the chart? If not, ask a classmate or look up the word. Then fill in the chart with the noun forms.

VERB	NOUN
devote	
achieve	
distribute	
demonstrate	
promote	
quote	
involve	
restore	
erode	
persist	

2. Choose one of the words above to complete the following sentences. The meaning of the word you need is in parentheses. (You may need to change verb forms.)

   a. I told the reporter not to (repeat words exactly) ________________ me in his newspaper article.

   b. So much (loss of soil from the earth's surface) ________________ had occurred that there wasn't enough ground cover to hold the tree roots securely.

   c. Is it possible to (bring back to an original condition) ________________ your trust in someone after you have lost it?

   d. His (dedication; loyalty) ________________ to his children was clear.

   e. She should be proud of her (successes) ________________.

   f. Maathai's work (shows) ________________ how individuals can make a difference little by little.

   g. If you (continue steadily without giving up) ________________ in your studies, you're likely to succeed.

h. Some people believe that wealth should be (divided up; spread out) ________________ more equally.

i. Her (participation; preoccupation) ________________ in politics sometimes caused problems for her family.

j. His organization (supports, often for the public good) ________________ the idea of increased mass transportation to reduce the city's dependence on oil.

ACTIVITY 13 USING VOCABULARY

Read the following conversation and fill in the blanks with the vocabulary below. Use each word only once. Then listen and check your answers.

*benefits**	*devoted**	*globally**	*impact**	*intentions*	*persist**

John: I just saw the movie that Al Gore, Jr. made, *An Inconvenient Truth*. That man is really ________ (1.) to educating people about global warming. Have you seen the movie?

Mari: I have. It made quite a(n) ________ (2.) on me. It really made me rethink the way I do things. Since then, I've been trying to change some of my energy use habits.

John: In what ways?

Mari: Well, for one thing, I've started biking instead of using my car for local errands. It's not a huge action, but every little bit matters. Like they say, "Think ________ (3.) act locally." And you know, I realize that if I ________ (4.), I'll probably feel additional ________ (5.) from biking .... better health ... so it's a "win-win" situation.

John: How's it going?

Mari: Well, my ________ (6.) are good but sometimes I'm in a rush and I still use my car.

John: One step at a time, I guess.

Mari: True. And what about you? Did the movie change your thinking or behavior?

ACTIVITY 14 RETAINING VOCABULARY

VOCABULARY LEARNING STRATEGY

A good way to remember a new word is to *use* it in a meaningful way.

The questions below use vocabulary from this unit. Work with a partner to ask and answer each of these questions with true information about yourself.

1. Some people are devoted to their work, their studies, their family, their art. What are you devoted to?
2. People often leave specific possessions to specific people in their will. For example, they might choose to leave a special ring to a sister or daughter. Talk about specific items that you'd leave to specific people in your will.
3. What have been some important changes in your life in the preceding year?
4. Have you ever resigned from a job? If so, why? If not, what would cause you to consider resigning?
5. Tell about something you have done that required persistence.

ACTIVITY 15 BEYOND THE LECTURE: READING, WRITING, SPEAKING

1. Go to the official Web site of the Nobel Prize organization (http://www.nobelprize.org).

   Read about another winner of the Nobel Prize. Be prepared to speak for 3 minutes to your classmates about the person you've read about. (There are numerous links at the site, including links to each winner's biography, Nobel lecture, photos, and interviews.)

2. Each year Nobel Committees send invitations to thousands of members of academies, university professors, scientists, previous Nobel Laureates, members of parliamentary assemblies, and others, asking them to submit candidates for the Nobel Prizes for the coming year. Write a letter to the Nobel Committee nominating someone for one of the prizes, supporting your nomination with facts.

3. Watch the movie *An Inconvenient Truth*. Write a movie review, rating the movie "Excellent," "Very Good," "Good," "Fair," or "Poor." Support your evaluation with specific reasons.

LISTENING FOR ORGANIZATION (PART 2)

7

Goals

- Follow three more organizational plans used by lecturers: describing characteristics, describing a process or sequence of events, and classifying
- Understand and follow the cues that signal these organizational plans
- Listen to and take notes on lectures using these organizational plans
- Practice using notes to answer various test-type questions

In Unit 6, you practiced recognizing and taking notes using three organizational plans: defining, listing, and exemplifying. In this unit, you will learn about and practice three more plans.

DISCUSSION

Teaching Others

1. Talk about some different methods that people have used to teach you skills or knowledge. Think about teachers in school, parents and family members, coaches, and friends. Which methods were the most/least successful for you? the most/least enjoyable?
2. Think about a skill or subject area you know well. Imagine that you are going to teach it to a small class. What steps would you take? How much planning would you do? What would you do first?
3. Are you an auditory learner, learning best by listening? a visual learner, learning best by seeing something? a tactile learner, learning best by touching something? a kinesthetic learner, learning best by doing? Give examples from your experience.
4. How might these ideas relate to organization in lectures?

Describing Characteristics

In this case, the lecturer's goal is to describe an object or living thing through its characteristics. In particular, the lecturer focuses on the object's physical qualities and setting.

Notes from a lecture using this pattern might look like this:

Moon's highlands
- dominated by craters
  - craters range in size: up to 150 miles
- extend 100s of miles
- up to 3.5 miles above lowlands

CUES TO RECOGNIZE DESCRIPTIONS

Sometimes lecturers present descriptions without any cues. Other times, lecturers use some of the words or phrases below to signal the description.

1. Phrases or sentences describing an object's characteristics:

   Concerning X's appearance, …
   Let's look at X's physical makeup.
   X is made up of …
   The layout of X is …

2. Phrases referring to sensory perception:

   X { *acts* / *feels* / *smells* / *sounds* / *tastes* } *like …*

   If we were to visit (see / draw / examine / x-ray, etc.) X, we would see …

3. Analogies:

   X is spiderlike (humanlike, etc.).
   Like a river …

4. Prepositions of place (and other terms) describing position:

above	*under*	*adjacent to*	*up there*
below	*next to*	*across from*	*down here*
on	*diagonal(ly)*	*on the right/left*	
in	*vertical(ly)*	*in the back/front/center*	
over	*horizontal(ly)*	*in the foreground/background*	

5. Rhetorical questions preceding descriptions:

   What does X look (act / feel) like?

Exercise 1

You will hear three lecture excerpts that include descriptions. Read the information about each excerpt. Then, while listening, write as many descriptive details as you can.

Example

Excerpt from a human anatomy lecture

VOCABULARY

cardiac: (medical term) related to the heart
branched: divided into two or more directions

Classes of muscle

Item — 1. Cardiac muscle

Description — –Striated (looks like lines run thru, not smooth)
–Branched (like freeway system)

1. Excerpt from a lecture on ecology

VOCABULARY

shrub: a bush; a woody plant

Item — Typical deciduous woodland

Description

(continued on next page)

2. Excerpt from a lecture on human development

VOCABULARY
limb: an arm or leg

Item	2nd mo. of embryo development
Description	

3. Excerpt from the same lecture on human development

Item	4th – 5th mo. of fetal development
Description	

B Describing a Process or Sequence of Events

In this case, the lecturer's goal is to demonstrate how something unfolded over time by organizing information according to a process or sequence of events.

Notes from a lecture organized as a process might look like this:

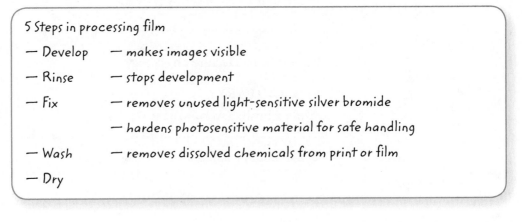

5 Steps in processing film

— Develop	— makes images visible
— Rinse	— stops development
— Fix	— removes unused light-sensitive silver bromide
	— hardens photosensitive material for safe handling
— Wash	— removes dissolved chemicals from print or film
— Dry	

Notes from a lecture organized as a sequence of events might look like this:

Film History:

- 1820s Joseph Niepce & Louis Daguerre—tried find method to make photo
- 1829 Joseph Niepce: created "heliograph"
- 1839 Louis Daguerre: created "daguerreotype"-
  - needed 15 min. exposure
  - made positive images ∴ no copies
- 1887 Hannibal Goodwin: invented film & film roll
- George Eastman: perfected film, mass marketed

CUES TO RECOGNIZE A PROCESS OR SEQUENCE OF EVENTS

1. Time expressions signaling a sequence of events or steps in a process:

   First (Second / Third), …
   Next (Then / Subsequently / Later / After that), …
   Prior to (Previously / Before that), …
   Formerly,
   At first, …
   In 2011 (In the first century / In the intervening years), …
   Initially …
   During (By the end of) the first month …

2. Phrases or sentences signaling a sequence of events or steps in a process:

   In order to arrive at this point, we had to …
   So far, I've mentioned three stages of development.
   We can trace the development …
   These are a set or series of actions that take place in a certain order …
   These are the steps …

   Let's look at {
   how this came about.
   where this comes from.
   how to X.
   (the steps involved in) this process.
   }

3. Rhetorical questions signaling a description of a process or sequence of events:

   What exactly causes this precipitation?
   How can we achieve this combination?
   What led up to the outbreak of war?
   How did this come to pass?

Exercise 2

You will hear three lecture excerpts that include descriptions of processes or sequences of events. First read the information about each excerpt. Then, while listening to the excerpts, take notes in the spaces provided.

Example
Excerpt from a lecture by Carl Sagan on global community

Heading	All humans come from same area — E. Africa
Sequence	species Homo sapiens began there — a few 100,000 yrs. ago
	human family " " " — " " million " "
	initially — small group — family members
	— wandering
	— following game
	— #s — few
	— powers — feeble
	intervening yrs. — humans expanded to every continent
	— incl. oceans & space!
	Now — 5.6 bill. humans
	— awesome powers!

1. Excerpt from a lecture on human development

VOCABULARY
blood vessels: veins through which blood flows

Heading	Embryonic period
Sequence	1st mo.
	by end of 1st mo.
	2nd mo.

2. Excerpt from a lecture on the spread of the plague

VOCABULARY

epidemic: many cases of a disease that spreads quickly
pandemic: an epidemic spread over a very wide area
medieval times: A.D. 1000–1500, the Middle Ages
outbreak: a sudden appearance of a disease

Heading	3 great pandemics of plague in recorded history
Sequence	1st
	2nd
	3rd

3. Excerpt from a lecture on social psychology

VOCABULARY

norm: an accepted or expected standard of behavior or thinking among a given group of people

Heading	Rituals — set or series of actions taking place in certain order — form norm e.g., Argyle (British psychol.) identified steps in "new neighbor ritual" (when new fam. moves into neighborhood)
Sequence	1.
	2.
	3.
	4.
	5.
	6.
	7.
Conclusion	Knowledge of rituals makes us skillful in given society

C Classifying Subtopics

In this case, the lecturer's goal is to make a topic more manageable by creating categories to organize the information from the larger topic.

A *classification* provides headings so that information can be grouped together based on similar characteristics. For example, a musicologist may present a lecture on different types of musical instruments by talking about string, wind, and percussion instruments. If the lecture compared the types while describing them, this would be a combination of a classification organizational plan and a comparison/contrast organizational plan.

Notes from a lecture presenting a classification might look like this:

Edward Hall's Classification of Cultures

Low-Context Cultures

— more attention given to message or event than to context of event

i.e., message/event has meaning in itself

e.g., German, Swiss cultures

High-Context Cultures

— more attention paid to context of message or event than to message itself

i.e., more important who you are, your family connections, than words

e.g., Arab, Greek cultures

Alternatively, these notes might be organized in columns:

Edward Hall's Classification of Cultures

<u>Low-Context Cultures</u>	<u>High-Context Cultures</u>
— more attention given to messages or event than to context of event	— more attention paid to context of message or event than to message itself
i.e., message/event has meaning in itself	i.e., more important who you are, your family connections, than words
e.g., German, Swiss cultures	e.g., Arab, Greek cultures

CUES TO RECOGNIZE CLASSIFICATIONS

1. Phrases indicating categories or divisions:

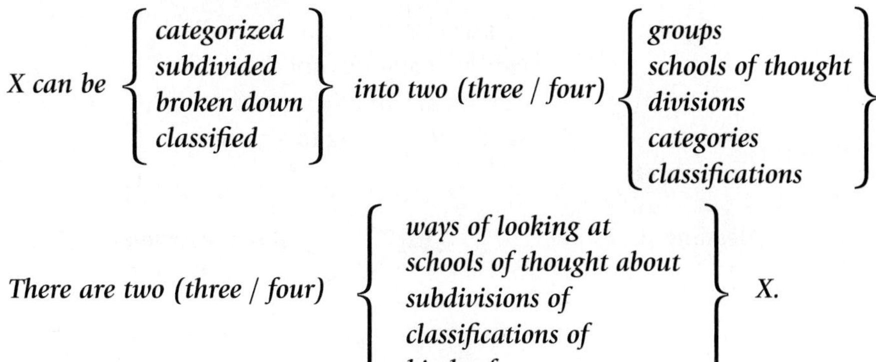

X can be {*categorized* / *subdivided* / *broken down* / *classified*} *into two (three / four)* {*groups* / *schools of thought* / *divisions* / *categories* / *classifications*}.

There are two (three / four) {*ways of looking at* / *schools of thought about* / *subdivisions of* / *classifications of* / *kinds of*} *X.*

We're going to address two types of change … The first type is …

We can think about memory systems as … or …

2. Rhetorical questions signaling classifications:

How many different kinds of X are there?
What are some ways in which we can look at X?
How can X be classified (categorized)?

Exercise 3

You will hear three lecture excerpts that include classifications. Read the information about each excerpt. Then, while listening to the excerpts, take notes in the spaces provided.

Example
Excerpt from a psychology lecture

VOCABULARY

in retrospect: looking backwards
acute: strong, serious, severe

Heading	CHANGE	
Classifications	GRADUAL APPROACH	ACUTE APPROACH
	Takes time Often safer Often notice in retrospect Primary way to change Most common	immed. sudden change: still takes prep.
	Neither QUICK FIX!	

(continued on next page)

1. Excerpt from a lecture on memory

VOCABULARY

unconscious: not aware or realizing
rigid: unchanging; not flexible
reflex: an automatic reaction
procedural: relating to a process

Heading	Memory systems
Classifications	Implicit memories / Explicit memories

2. Excerpt from an anthropology lecture on the evolution of human emotions

VOCABULARY

drive: motivation

Heading	3 Brain systems—evolving fr. mating & reproduction
Classifications	1. 2. 3.

3. Excerpt from a lecture on family systems

VOCABULARY

compensation: payment for a service or loss

Term	Marriage payment — most common in arranged marriages
Definition	— Alliance betw. families to compensate other for work & reproductive potential
Heading	Types of payments:
Classifications	— — —

LECTURE 7

Paging Robodoc: Robots in Medicine (Biology/Technology)

Vocabulary

Related to Surgery

Check (✓) the words you know. Underline the words you want to learn. Then check their meaning with your instructor or in a dictionary.

surgery
anesthesiologist
surgeon
- *cardiac surgeon*
- *neurosurgeon*
- *orthopedic surgeon*
- *pediatric surgeon*

operating room
operating table

scalpel
incision

imaging tools:
CT (computer tomography) scan
MRI (magnetic resonance imaging) scan

to excise a tumor
to set a bone
to suture / stitch
to transplant
to implant
to anesthetize

The doctor is ready to see you.

ACTIVITY 1 PRE-LECTURE READING AND DISCUSSION

Discuss the following in small groups.

1. In the past 100 years, what have been some of the major advances in medical treatment? Consider drugs, scientific knowledge, technology, and so on.
2. Read the article on the next page. Then discuss your answers to the questions that follow.

Cybersurgery[1]

Computers, Cameras, and Robots are Creating an Improved Operating System for Doctors

Jane E. Stevens, *Los Angeles Times*

Colonel Richard Satava has a vision for medicine. He sees it shifting its focus from blood and guts to bits and bytes.[2] Satava, program manager for advanced medical technologies at the Defense Department's Advanced Research Projects Agency, has been a driving[3] force in bringing virtual reality[4] to medicine, where computers create a "virtual" or simulated[5] environment for surgeons and other medical practitioners.

"With virtual reality we'll be able to put a surgeon in every foxhole,"[6] said Satava, a U.S. Army surgeon. He envisions a time when soldiers who are wounded fighting overseas are put in mobile surgical units equipped with computers.

The computers would transmit images of the soldiers to surgeons back in the U.S. The surgeons would look at the soldier through virtual reality helmets that contain a small screen displaying the image of the wound and cover the eyes to block out the real world. The doctors would use their hands to guide robotic instruments in the battlefield mobile surgical unit that operate on the soldier.

Although Satava's vision may be years away from standard operating procedure, scientists are progressing toward virtual reality surgery. Engineers at SRI International in Palo Alto [California] are developing a tele[7]-operating device. As surgeons watch a three-dimensional[8] image of the surgery, they move instruments that are connected to a computer, which passes their movements to robotic instruments that perform the surgery. The computer provides feedback to the surgeon on force, textures, and sound.

These technological wonders may not yet be part of the community hospital setting, but increasingly some of the machinery is finding its way into civilian[9] medicine. At Wayne State University Medical School, neurosurgeon Lucia Zamorano takes images of the brain from state-of-the-art magnetic resonance (MRI)[10] and computer tomography (CT) scans and uses a computer program to produce a 3-D image. She can then maneuver[11] the 3-D image on the computer screen to map the shortest, least invasive[12] surgical path to the tumor.[13] Zamorano is also using technology that attaches a probe[14] to surgical instruments so that she can track their positions. While excising[15] a tumor deep in the brain, she watches the movement of her surgical tools in a computer graphics image of the patient's brain taken before surgery.

During endoscopic procedures—operations that are done through small incisions[16] in the body in which a miniature camera and surgical tools are maneuvered—surgeons are wearing 3-D glasses for a better view. And they are commanding robot surgeons to cut away tissue more accurately than human surgeons can.

Satava says, "We are in the midst[17] of a fundamental change in the field of medicine."

[1] *cyber-:* (prefix) referring to electronic and computerized communication systems (e.g., cyberspace, cybernetics)
[2] *bits and bytes:* units of measurement for computer data
[3] *driving:* motivating
[4] *virtual reality:* a world that seems like reality, created through a computer
[5] *simulate:* to imitate something
[6] *foxhole:* a hole in the ground where soldiers protect themselves
[7] *tele-:* (prefix) far (e.g., telephone, television)
[8] *three-dimensional (3D):* having height, width, and depth
[9] *civilian:* nonmilitary
[10] *MRI and CT scans:* machinery used to take internal body images
[11] *maneuver:* to control and move; to handle
[12] *invasive:* relating to entering and cutting into the body
[13] *tumor:* a growth of diseased tissue
[14] *probe:* a tool used to explore inside something
[15] *excise:* to remove (usually by cutting)
[16] *incision:* a narrow cut in the skin
[17] *midst:* middle (of a place or activity)

a. Who is Richard Satava? What is his vision of medical treatment in the future?

b. Find examples in the article of current medical uses for computers, cameras, and robots.

c. The article ends with Satava's quote: "We are in the midst of a fundamental change in the field of medicine." Why is this a *fundamental* change? Considering the past, what other changes in medicine would you classify as equally fundamental—that is, changing the field in the most basic and significant ways?

3. Have you (or someone you know) had any experiences with medical technology? If so, describe the experiences.

ACTIVITY 2 PREPARING FOR THE LECTURE

The title of the lecture is "Paging Robodoc: Robots in Medicine." When you hear the word *robot*, what do you imagine? What do you expect the lecturer to tell you about robots in medicine? Brainstorm ideas with your classmates.

Listen to the introduction. Then mark the statements below *T* (True) or *F* (False).

F 1. The lecturer will talk more about robots that look human.

T 2. The lecturer will talk more about robots in many different fields, one of which is medicine.

F 3. The lecturer will talk more about robots in one particular area—the hospital operating room.

F 4. The lecturer will talk more about movie and TV images of robots.

T 5. The lecturer will talk more about what a robot is.

ACTIVITY 3 LISTENING FOR THE LARGER PICTURE

Read the following questions before the lecture begins. Then listen to the lecture once without taking notes. After listening, answer the questions.

1. The lecturer's goal is to tell the audience something about robots in medicine. This is a broad topic, so the lecturer covers only some aspects of the topic. Which of the following does the lecturer do? Check (✓) the appropriate column.

	YES	NO
a. defines *robot*	✓	
b. provides historical background about the use of robots in hospitals		✓
c. explains the essential parts of a robot		✓
d. gives an example of one particular use of robots in hospitals, Robodoc	✓	
e. gives numerous examples of robots used in hospitals		✓
f. classifies different types of hospital-based robots		✓
g. describes the process of how Robodoc works	✓	
h. speaks about some people's resistance or fears about robots in the operating room	✓	

2. To explore the use of robots in the operating room, hip surgery was an obvious choice. Why? Check (✓) the appropriate column.

	YES	NO
a. it is a physically laborious type of surgery		
b. it is performed infrequently		
c. it is performed frequently		
d. it is more accurate when done with robotic assistance		
e. it is cheaper when done with robotic assistance		

ACTIVITY 4 ORGANIZATION

Read this summary of the lecture organization.

The lecture primarily demonstrates three organizational plans:

- *defining a term:* The lecturer begins by defining *robot* and then gives information about the essential components of robots (the microprocessor, an arm with five or six joints, and the end effector).
- *exemplifying a topic:* The lecturer details one example of the use of robots in hospitals: Robodoc, a robot used in hip replacement surgery.
- *describing a surgical process:* The lecturer explains why robots are particularly suited for this type of surgery and describes the surgical process.

The lecturer concludes by mentioning some expressed concerns about robots in the operating room but generally emphasizes the potential of robots.

What do you remember about the definition and components of robots? About robotic use in surgery? Discuss with a partner.

ACTIVITY 5 DEFINING VOCABULARY

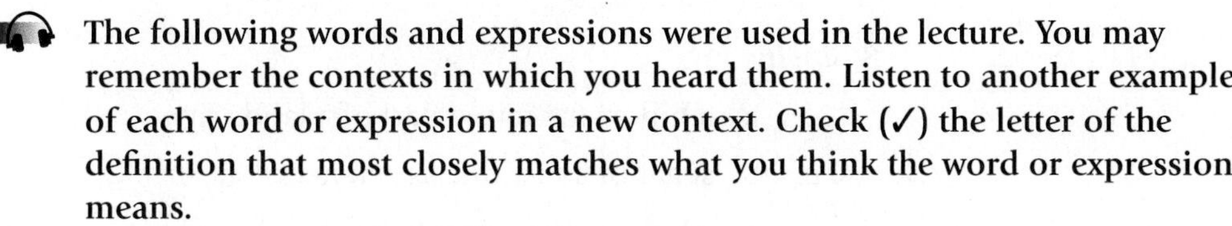

The following words and expressions were used in the lecture. You may remember the contexts in which you heard them. Listen to another example of each word or expression in a new context. Check (✓) the letter of the definition that most closely matches what you think the word or expression means.

1. *labor**

   ___ **a.** fear, especially relating to responsibilities

   ___ **b.** work, especially tiring, physical work

   _✓_ **c.** love, especially familial love

2. *manipulate*

   _✓_ **a.** to win a race easily

   ___ **b.** to fly a plane or other airborne vehicle

   ___ **c.** to handle or control skillfully

3. *task**

   ___ **a.** a question; something needing an answer

   ___ **b.** a child of any age

   _✓_ **c.** a duty; a piece of work that must be done

(continued on next page)

4. *alter**

___ a. to lose weight; to go on a diet

___ b. to change; to make different

___ c. to throw something useless away

5. *precision**

___ a. education

___ b. tension; anxiety

___ c. exactness

6. *steady*

___ a. firm; sure in position or movement

___ b. dirty; unclean

___ c. easily moved or shifted

7. *lose one's grip*

___ a. to lose an argument

___ b. to lose or loosen a tight hold

___ c. to lose sight of

8. *cavity*

___ a. a hill or the raised part of a landscape

___ b. sugar or substitute sweeteners

___ c. a hole or the empty space inside a mass

9. *glimpse*

___ a. a quick look

___ b. a short visit

___ c. an autograph

10. *expose**

___ a. to burn

___ b. to uncover (to the air, cold, etc.)

___ c. to stand in a fixed position for lengthy periods

In addition to these words, the lecturer also uses certain terms for various body parts, tools, materials, and mechanical processes. Check the meaning of the following terms: *femur, mallet, chisel, cement, bore (a hole)*, and *carve (a shape)*.

ACTIVITY 6 LISTENING AND NOTE-TAKING

Listen to the lecture a second time and take notes.

Introduction

Definition of robot

What is a robot? How used in our world today
Operating room (hospital)
Check to forsed labor, work for us, asisting us

can perform a variety of tasks

Essential components of robots

Robot - reprogramable, multifunctional manipulator design to move things
Programe it to do diff things / kind of machine
How work? Microprocessor (activate dif. movements of robot)
Effector

Single arm
Hand
Some have 2 fingers hand

Example of robots

Robots in hospitals: e.g., Robodoc Not neces. smart
Endeffector
First generation tech. in medicine
Surgery

Replacement surgery
Hipoplacement surgery

Reasons for use in hip surgery

Why esp. useful for hip surgery?
Physically demended

Process

How Robodoc works
Potion come in, scane (3 picture bone), surg. sit down on a comp., choose implant, the best for potion
Operation room, surg. makes instidion
Size, shape, location of the implant (rob. work)
Full control over the robot (takes 20 min)
Rob. good where surgeres are not so good

Conclusions

Robots will replace Surg.
Rob. going crazy
will devel. assist surg
Now we can imagine changes
Can give us a glives future might be

ACTIVITY  REPLAY QUESTION

Listen to an excerpt from the lecture and answer the following question.

Why does the lecturer mention Apple computers? Check (✓) two answers.

____ a. The lecturer is talking about Robodoc's Apple-designed microprocessor.

____ b. The lecturer wants to say that Robodoc is in an early stage of development.

____ c. The lecturer is making an analogy, saying that Robodoc is to medical robots as Apple's first computers were to microcomputers.

____ d. The lecturer wants to say that Robodoc is as "user-friendly" as Apple computers.

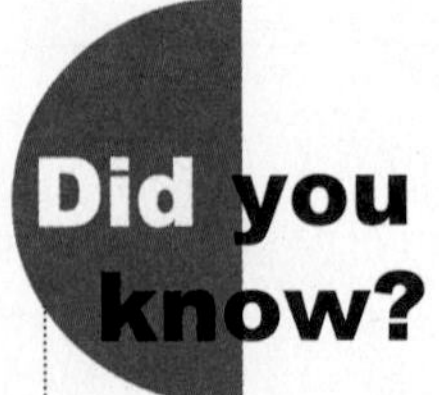

A robot shaped like a human being is called an android.

ACTIVITY  "OTHER VOICES" FOLLOW-UP

1. The professor is telling the class about a South African athlete, Oscar Pistorius. After listening, check (✓) whether the professor mentions these facts about Pistorius.

	YES	NO
a. He was born without legs.		
b. His legs were amputated[1] when he was very young.		
c. He learned to walk and run with prosthetic devices.[2]		
d. He wanted to compete in the Olympics.		
e. Some athletes complained because they didn't think he was good enough for the Olympic team.		
f. Some people felt that his "high-tech" limbs gave him an advantage over other runners		
g. He was allowed to compete in the qualifying trials[3] for the 2008 Olympics.		
h. He didn't "make the cut"[4] for the 2008 Olympics.		
i. He uses performance-enhancing drugs[5] (e.g., steroids).		

LISTENING AND NOTE-TAKING STRATEGIES

1. Review your notes as soon as possible after listening, adding information that you remember but didn't note.
2. Ask classmates for specific pieces of information that you might have missed.
3. Rewrite your notes soon after listening to add information that you remember and to emphasize information and connections between ideas.

[1] *amputate:* to cut off surgically

[2] *prosthetic device:* an artificial limb (arm, leg, hand); a prosthesis

[3] *qualifying trial:* a competition to judge who is fit or ready and limit the number of competitors

[4] *"make the cut":* to stay in the group after a qualifying trial or test

[5] *performance-enhancing drugs:* drugs that improve or add to one's performance

2. The professor then asks students to discuss the issues that Pistorius's story raises. Listen to one group's conversation. Of the four students in this group,
   - how many support the idea of athletes like Pistorius competing in the Olympics if they qualify? ______
   - how many oppose the idea? ______
   - how many would rather not make this kind of decision? ______

Oscar Pistorius

ACTIVITY 9 POST-LECTURE READING AND DISCUSSION

Discuss the following in small groups.

1. In the lecture, the speaker notes surgeons' concerns and patients' fears. Do you have any fears about the new technologies in medicine? If so, what are they?

2. Robodoc is not alone. Read the article on the next page from *Discover*, a magazine about science and technology, to learn about another robotic surgeon. When you have finished, discuss your answers to the questions that follow.

Robotic Surgery

Surgeons make big incisions because they need to get their hands in the body. But with tiny robotic hands, their incisions would be smaller—and less traumatic.[1]

Kathy A. Svitil, *Discover*

Since it was developed over a decade ago, laparoscopic surgery—in which instruments are inserted through small incisions—has been used by surgeons whenever possible. Patients are less traumatized, require shorter hospital stays, and heal faster than with conventional[2] surgery. Yet despite these benefits, laparoscopy is a challenging procedure. "Surgeons find it hard," says Shankar Sastry, an electrical engineer at the University of California at Berkeley. "It's like operating with chopsticks."

Indeed, laparoscopic instruments are mainly limited to scissors, staplers (to close incisions or attach blood vessels), and graspers[3] (to manipulate[4] tissue). The instruments enter the body through a long tube; a video image from a tiny camera called an endoscope poked[5] through another incision guides the surgeon.

For a relatively simple procedure like gallbladder removal, the tools work well enough. But surgeons can't use the instruments to perform complicated tasks like suturing[6] and knot tying. Because of these limitations, says Sastry, most operations can't be performed endoscopically.

However, now Sastry and his Berkeley colleagues have developed laparoscopic tools—including miniature robotic hands with the dexterity[7] to tie knots. "The reason you have to cut a person open is to get the surgeon's hands in there," he says. "But if you can get little instruments in there that let the surgeons feel as if they are working with their hands in a normal procedure, you don't have to have a big incision."

The Berkeley system consists of a pencil-size joystick (one each for the surgeon's right and left hands), a computer, and right-hand and left-hand end effectors—the robotic instruments that snake[8] into the body to perform the actual surgery. In early models, these resembled three-fingered hands. Now each hydraulically[9] powered end effector consists of a single digit,[10] three to four inches long and less than half an inch wide. It has four joints that rotate and swing back and forth and a grasper at the end. The result: a finger that functions like an entire hand.

To operate, a surgeon—who can be in the same room as the patient or at a remote[11] location—uses the joysticks just as he would normal surgical instruments. A computer program translates the surgeon's motions into the movements of the end effectors.

The system also has force feedback, which relays[12] to doctors the response of muscles and other tissues to their actions. The feedback makes the procedure feel more like normal surgery. The research team is also working on tactile sensors that will transmit the feel of tissue to the surgeon's fingertips.

"The overall goal," says Sastry, "is pretty lofty:[13] to not cut a person open unless there is just nothing else to do—for instance, if you have to replace a hip, there is no choice but to go in there and remove the old hip—but in every instance to make sutures and cuts that are as small as possible."

1 *traumatic:* shocking or painful (to the body or mind)
2 *conventional:* traditional
3 *grasp:* to hold on tightly
4 *manipulate:* to handle; to change the position of something
5 *poke:* to press, as with a finger or stick
6 *suture:* to sew up a wound
7 *dexterity:* skill or ability (with one's hands)
8 *snake:* to wind
9 *hydraulic:* using water or other fluids
10 *digit:* a finger or toe
11 *remote:* distant
12 *relay:* to communicate; to pass on information
13 *lofty:* elevated; high

a. What is laparoscopic surgery?

b. What are the advantages of laparoscopic surgery?

c. What are the limitations and challenges of traditional laparoscopic surgery?

d. What system have Sastry and his colleagues developed? What are the components of their system? How does the surgeon operate with it?

ACTIVITY 10 USING YOUR NOTES

Use your notes to answer the following questions. Use your own paper.

1. According to the Robot Industries Association, what is the definition of the term *robot*?

2. True or False?

    ___ a. The word *robot* comes from a Czech word meaning "human-like."

    ___ b. According to the Robot Industries Association's definition of a robot, a robot may or may not be reprogrammable.

    ___ c. The end effector of a robot looks exactly like a human hand.

    ___ d. Hip replacement surgery is pretty uncommon.

    ___ e. When hip surgery is done manually, surgeons have to carve a cavity and drill holes in a patient's femur.

    ___ f. Robodoc doesn't actually drill a cavity into the patient's bone; Robodoc just tells the surgeon where to drill.

    ___ g. During Robodoc-assisted hip replacement surgery, the surgeon never actually goes near the patient except to do CT scans.

3. Why have surgeons traditionally needed to use cement to hold the hip implant in place? What has been a disadvantage of the cement?

4. Discuss the benefits of hip replacement surgery done by Robodoc as compared to traditional surgical techniques.

5. Describe the sequence of steps taken when Robodoc is used for hip replacement surgery.

ACTIVITY 11 COMPARING IDEAS

1. Compare your answers to Activity 10 with a partner or group. If you have different answers, check your notes and discuss your reasons for making your choices.

2. Compare your rewritten notes to the sample rewritten notes in Appendix D. Notice the organization. Is yours similar or different? Are your notes equally effective in making important ideas stand out?

ACTIVITY 12 ACADEMIC WORD LIST VOCABULARY

Match the word and its meaning. Write the correct letter in the space provided. Examples are given to help you see words in context.

Group 1

a. a picture
b. a measurement of something (e.g., height, length, width)
c. a class of objects with similar characteristics formed at the same time, sharing history and development
d. state of being unprotected from something

___ 1. ***exposure*** Limit your exposure to X-rays and other radiation.

___ 2. ***image*** The photographic image isn't clear because I couldn't hold the camera steady.

___ 3. ***generation*** First-generation computers were big and slow compared to the new generation.

___ 4. ***dimension*** Before ordering a rug, make sure you know the dimensions of the room.

Group 2

a. to send; to pass from one to another
b. to keep or maintain possession of
c. to experience (often something negative or difficult)
d. to help or aid

___ 5. ***assist*** The nurse assisted the doctor in the operating room.

___ 6. ***retain*** I can't retain all that information; it's too much to remember.

___ 7. ***transmit*** You can't transmit AIDS through casual contact.

___ 8. ***undergo*** She needs to undergo surgery tomorrow.

Group 3

a. suitable
b. provided with supplies or purposeful items
c. not logical
d. changeable

___ 9. ***appropriate*** It isn't appropriate to wear shorts to the office. They're too casual.

___ 10. ***irrational*** His irrational behavior made people wonder if he needed psychiatric help.

___ 11. ***variable*** Springtime weather is very variable; you never know what to expect.

___ 12. ***equipped*** The car is equipped with a stereo and CD changer.

ACTIVITY 13 USING VOCABULARY

 **You will hear vocabulary from the lecture, reading, and discussion in different contexts. Listen and check (✓) the letter of the closest paraphrase of the information.**

Group A

1. ___ a. It is necessary for carpenters to be strong.
   ___ b. It is necessary for carpenters to be exact.
   ___ c. It is necessary for carpenters to be creative.

2. ___ a. I know a carpenter who uses power tools for large tasks and hand tools for more detail-oriented tasks.
   ___ b. I know a carpenter who doesn't use power tools at all.
   ___ c. I know a carpenter who uses power tools for even the smallest details.

3. ___ a. I spent a long time with him in his workshop, and I was surprised at how much physical work was involved in his work.
   ___ b. I passed by and noticed him in his workshop, and I was surprised at how quiet his workshop was.
   ___ c. I passed by and noticed him in his workshop, and I was surprised at how much physical work was involved in his work.

Group B

1. ___ a. My doctor recommended a brain surgeon to me.
   ___ b. My doctor recommended a bone surgeon to me.
   ___ c. My doctor recommended a heart surgeon to me.

2. ___ a. The specialist told me that my operation would require a very tiny cut.
   ___ b. The specialist told me that my operation would take a very short time.
   ___ c. The specialist told me that I had to make a quick decision about my operation.

Group C

1. ___ a. Mountain climbing requires strength.
   ___ b. Mountain climbing requires a firm grip.
   ___ c. Mountain climbing requires fearlessness.

2. ___ a. Most mountain climbers use ropes in case they lose hold of the rock.
   ___ b. Most mountain climbers use ropes to pull themselves up the rock.
   ___ c. Most mountain climbers use ropes to help other climbers.

(continued on next page)

Group D

1. ____ a. I have a simple test for you.
   ____ b. I have a simple job for you.
   ____ c. I have a simple question for you.

2. ____ a. Type a letter on the computer exactly as you see it.
   ____ b. Type a letter on the computer, making corrections as you go along.
   ____ c. Type a letter on the computer as fast as you can.

3. ____ a. When you finish typing, exit the computer system.
   ____ b. When you finish typing, begin another letter.
   ____ c. When you finish typing, call me over.

ACTIVITY 14 RETAINING VOCABULARY

VOCABULARY STRATEGY

Learn derivative forms of words when you learn new words.

NOUNS	VERBS	ADJECTIVES
surgeon/surgery		*surgical*
operation	*to operate*	*operable/inoperable*
implant	*to implant*	
transplant	*to transplant*	
alteration	*to alter*	
manipulation	*to manipulate*	*manipulative*
precision		*precise/imprecise*
steadiness/unsteadiness	*to steady*	*steady/unsteady*
glimpse	*to glimpse*	
assistant/assistance	*to assist*	
transmission	*to transmit*	
retention	*to retain*	
variability/invariability/variation/variety	*to vary*	*variable/invariable/varied*
rationality/irrationality	*to rationalize*	*rational/irrational*
exposure	*to expose*	

Fill in the blanks with the correct form of the word. The first letters of the words are given as clues.

1. Doctors needed to o__________ to remove a tumor.
2. Eye surgery requires great p__________ and hand s__________.
3. The s__________ in the operating room asked for a__________ from one of the nurses.
4. Teachers can try to t__________ information to students but they can't control their r__________ of that information.
5. There is great v__________ in medical care in this city; be careful which hospital you go to.
6. The lawyer believed that someone had a__________ the patient's medical records.
7. Surgeons e__________ the patient's heart and then i__________ a device called "a pacemaker" to regulate her heartbeat.
8. The first human-to-human heart t__________ took place in South Africa in 1967.
9. The patient couldn't m__________ the eating utensils because his hand was so u__________.
10. The patient's i__________ answers provided a g__________ into his thought processes.

ACTIVITY 15 BEYOND THE LECTURE: WRITING

Write about one of the following topics.

1. What do you think medical care will be like 100 years from now? Use information from the lecture, articles, and your imagination to describe a hospital or medical center of the future. Consider some of the following questions: What will doctors' jobs be like? What will patient care be like? What will a hospital look like? How will surgical procedures change?
2. Describe an experience that you had with surgery or medical care. How much information did you have prior to undergoing the treatment? Did you have alternative treatments to consider? In retrospect, were your decisions about treatments, hospitals, and doctors the best ones? Since your experience, have there been innovations in the field that would have made your experience easier?

LECTURE 8

How To Look at Art (Art)

Vocabulary

Related to Art

Check (✓) the words you know. Underline the words you want to learn. Then check their meaning with your instructor or in a dictionary.

sculpture
printmaking

medium/media:
oil
charcoal
acrylic paint
pastel

canvas
easel
portrait
landscape
still life
abstract art

in/out of focus
focal point

composition
perspective
2-D (two-dimensional)
3-D (three-dimensional)

diagonal
horizontal
vertical
zigzag

rectangle, rectangular
triangle, triangular
circle, circular

texture

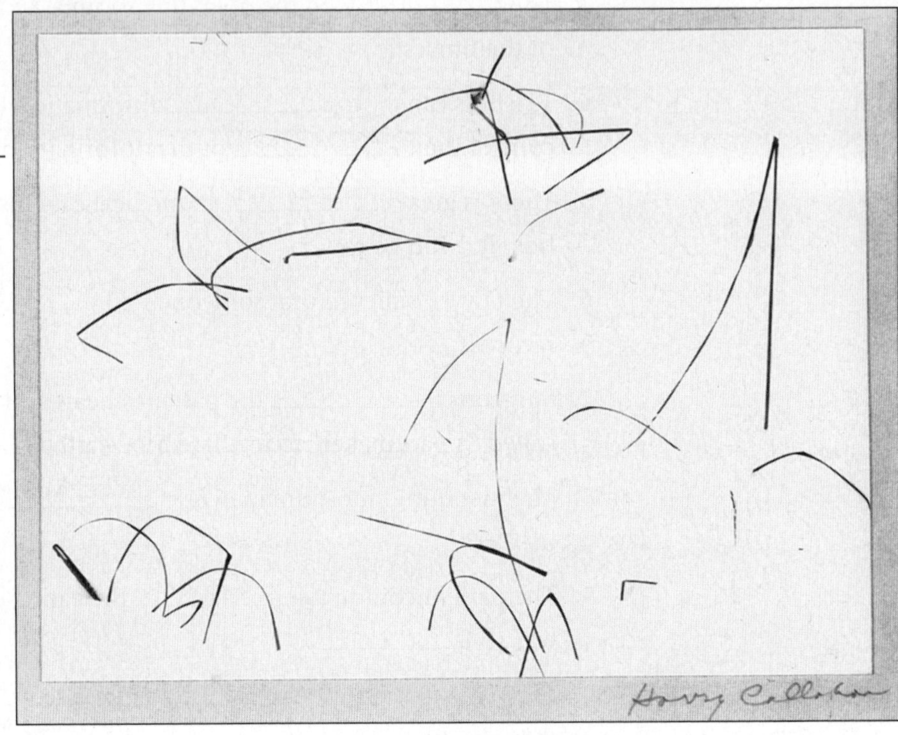

Harry Callahan (American, 1912–1999), Weeds in Snow, 1943. Gelatin silver print (photograph)

ACTIVITY 1 PRE-LECTURE DISCUSSION

Look at the artwork on this and the next page. Which ones do you like the best? The least? Rank them from 1 to 6, with 1 being your favorite.

____ Franz Kline, *Painting Number 2*
____ Vincent Van Gogh, *Corridor in the Asylum*
____ Dorothea Lange, *Migrant Mother, Nipomo, California*
____ Edgar Degas, *The Orchestra of the Opera*
____ Edward Hopper, *Early Sunday Morning*
____ Harry Callahan, *Weeds in Snow*

Liking a piece of art does not necessarily mean you would want to have it in your home. Which, if any, of these selections would you like to have in your home? Why? Which would you not like to have in your home? Why not?

Franz Kline (American, 1910–1962), Painting Number 2, *1954.*
Oil on canvas 6′8″ x 8′9″ (204.3 x 271.6 cm.)

Edgar Degas (French, 1834–1917), The Orchestra of the Opera, *1870.*
Oil on canvas, 22.2″ x 17.7″ (56.5 cm x 45 cm.)

Vincent Van Gogh (Dutch, 1853–1890), Corridor in the Asylum, *1889.*
Gouache and watercolor on paper, 24$\frac{1}{8}$″ x 18$\frac{5}{8}$″ (61.3 x 47.3 cm.)

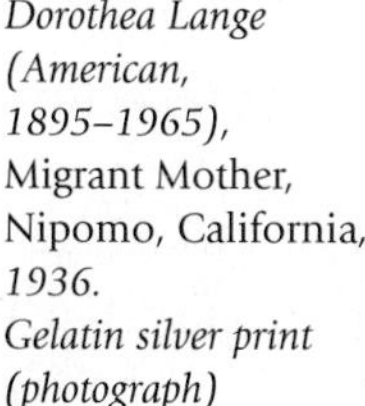

Dorothea Lange (American, 1895–1965), Migrant Mother, Nipomo, California, *1936.*
Gelatin silver print (photograph)

Edward Hopper (American, 1882–1967), Early Sunday Morning, *1930.*
Oil on canvas, 35″ x 60″ (88.9 x 152.4 cm.)

ACTIVITY 2 PREPARING FOR THE LECTURE

The title of the lecture is "How to Look at Art." How do you look at art? What do you expect the lecturer to tell you? Brainstorm ideas with your classmates.

Listen to the introduction. What does the lecturer plan to do?

___ **a.** give students ways to develop their intuitive[1] appreciation of art
___ **b.** give students ways to look at art more analytically[2] and systematically
___ **c.** give students historical background to help them understand artwork in its context
___ **d.** all of the above

What will the lecturer talk about next? ______________________

ACTIVITY 3 LISTENING FOR THE LARGER PICTURE

Read the following question before the lecture begins. Listen to the lecture once without taking notes. Then answer the question on a separate sheet of paper.

What is "directed looking" and what are its five components (categories of observation)?

ACTIVITY 4 ORGANIZATION

Read this summary of the lecture organization.

The lecture begins with a general overview of art appreciation. Then it uses three different organizational plans to explain "directed looking," a specific way of looking at art.

- *classifying a topic:* The lecturer explains directed looking by talking about five categories of observation.
- *exemplifying and describing characteristics:* Within each category, the lecturer gives examples and descriptions showing how one can apply this type of observation to a work of art.

What do you remember about each of the categories of observation and the examples given? Discuss with a partner.

---

[1] ***intuitive:*** able to understand without using logical reasoning

[2] ***analytical:*** having the ability to analyze (i.e., to examine critically and identify key elements)

ACTIVITY 5 DEFINING VOCABULARY

The following words and expressions were used in the lecture. You may remember the contexts in which you heard them. Listen to another example of each word or expression in a new context. Check (✓) the letter of the definition that most closely matches what you think the word or expression means.

1. *appreciation**
   ____ **a.** a sense of need
   ____ **b.** a sense of disappointment and sadness
   ____ **c.** a sense of understanding and enjoyment

2. *perspective**
   ____ **a.** historical sense
   ____ **b.** feeling of sadness
   ____ **c.** point of view

3. *on the contrary**
   ____ **a.** the opposite
   ____ **b.** a similar way
   ____ **c.** with certainty

4. *illusion*
   ____ **a.** something that is not what it seems to be
   ____ **b.** something that is a true representation of reality
   ____ **c.** something that costs a lot of money

5. *overlap**
   ____ **a.** to work overtime
   ____ **b.** to happen at the same time
   ____ **c.** to rise above; to be higher than

6. *apparent**
   ____ **a.** easily seen or understood
   ____ **b.** having responsibilities typical of a parent
   ____ **c.** upsetting or disturbing

7. *imply**
   ____ **a.** to express in an artistic manner
   ____ **b.** to express directly; to state clearly
   ____ **c.** to express indirectly; to suggest

8. *explicit**
   ____ **a.** unclear and partly expressed
   ____ **b.** clear and fully expressed
   ____ **c.** medically important and necessary

ACTIVITY 6 LISTENING AND NOTE-TAKING

 **Listen to the lecture a second time and take notes. Use your own paper, and follow the pattern below.**

Notice that this lecturer has a more participatory style than some other lecturers. Although the lecturer does the majority of speaking, he encourages students to add their ideas. As a note-taker, you need to listen to both the lecturer and the other students. Notice when the lecturer confirms the students' responses and consider whether there is important information to note.

Introduction	Directed looking
Definition/ explanation	
Classification of components of "directed looking" with examples and descriptions of each	5 cats. of observation: 1. 2.

ACTIVITY 7 REPLAY QUESTIONS

Listen to the introduction again and consider the lecturer's opinions.

1. What is the lecturer's attitude about having an intuitive reaction to art?

   ___ **a.** generally positive

   ___ **b.** neutral; neither positive nor negative

   ___ **c.** generally negative

   What did the lecturer say that makes you think this?

   ____

2. What is the lecturer's attitude about getting historical information about art?

   ___ **a.** generally positive

   ___ **b.** neutral; neither positive nor negative

   ___ **c.** generally negative

   What did the lecturer say that makes you think this?

   ____

LISTENING AND NOTE-TAKING STRATEGIES

1. Review your notes as soon as possible after listening, adding information that you remember but didn't note.
2. Ask classmates for specific pieces of information that you might have missed.
3. Rewrite your notes soon after listening to add information that you remember and to emphasize information and connections between ideas.

ACTIVITY 8 "OTHER VOICES" FOLLOW-UP

Two classmates, Jack and Jane, are talking after class. Listen to their conversation and answer the questions.

1. What is going to happen on Monday? Check (✓) the correct answer.

   ___ **a.** The teacher is giving a test on a photography exhibit at a museum.

   ___ **b.** The class is going off-campus to a museum exhibit.

   ___ **c.** A written and oral assignment about a photograph from the museum exhibit is due.

   ___ **d.** The teacher will be meeting individually with students in his office to discuss their assignment.

2. The teacher wants students to choose one photographic work from an exhibit and write about it from which three perspectives?

   ___ **a.** a "gut" (or intuitive) reaction

   ___ **b.** a "directed approach" analysis

   ___ **c.** a psychological perspective

   ___ **d.** a historical perspective

3. Which is true? Check (✓) the correct answer.

   ___ **a.** Students must carpool together to the exhibit.

   ___ **b.** Students must all go to the exhibit on the same day.

   ___ **c.** Students must attend the docent[1] tour.

   ___ **d.** Students must turn in a ticket stub if they don't go with the group.

4. How can we infer from the conversation that Jack is not a very good student?

   ____

[1] *docent:* a knowledgeable guide; especially through museums

ACTIVITY 9 POST-LECTURE READING AND DISCUSSION

Cave paintings have been found in Italy and France that are more than 30,000 years old.

Discuss the following in small groups.

1. Return to the artwork that you discussed before hearing the lecture. Using the technique of directed looking, analyze two works of art. (The lecturer comments about some aspects of each work but does not comment about every aspect of every work. Therefore, your group discussion should include *your* ideas based on directed looking as well as the lecturer's ideas.) When you have finished your discussion, present your ideas to the class.

2. Have you ever been to a museum and wondered how a piece of artwork got selected—why it was considered "good"? How do *you* decide if a piece of artwork is "good" or not?

3. Read the following from a book on ways to look at modern art.[1] What is this writer's criteria[2] for "good" art? Do you agree or disagree with this writer's view? In what ways?

The matter of aesthetic[1] quality is not simple. At any given moment, there may be a consensus[2] among curators,[3] artists, critics, dealers, and collectors that theoretically determines artistic merit,[4] but a look at history also shows that some things greatly admired later were scorned[5] when first introduced, and vice versa.[6]

For those who want to participate actively in debates on what makes a work "good," we need to create some parameters[7] by which to measure artistic success. My own fairly simple guideline is as follows: Art is a human-created expression that makes me think and feel at the same time. The thoughts and emotions it provokes are either new or different from the way I considered them before; they may tap into[8] something I only suspected or maybe did not know that I knew. Most important (and this is how I ultimately decide merit for myself), good art sustains[9] my interest over time, perhaps for its original appeal,[10] perhaps for reasons that are new each time I see it.

[1] ***aesthetic:*** related to appreciation of beauty
[2] ***consensus:*** agreement
[3] ***curator:*** a person in charge of a museum collection
[4] ***merit:*** quality, worth, value
[5] ***scorn:*** to look down on; to disrespect
[6] ***vice versa:*** the same in reverse
[7] ***parameters:*** limits that define an activity
[8] ***tap into:*** to get access or entry to
[9] ***sustain:*** to keep up or maintain (an activity)
[10] ***appeal:*** pleasing quality

---

[1] From Philip Yenawine, *How to Look at Modern Art*, Harry N. Abrams Inc., New York, 1991
[2] ***criteria:*** rules used to judge something

ACTIVITY 10 USING YOUR NOTES

Use your notes to answer the questions. Use your own paper for questions 2 through 5.

1. True or False?

    ___ **a.** A directed looking approach to art appreciation requires knowledge about the historical setting of the artwork.

    ___ **b.** The five categories of observation in a directed looking approach to art never overlap.

    ___ **c.** Abstract paintings never have a subject matter.

    ___ **d.** Typically, dark colors project and light ones recede.

2. Name the five categories of observation in a directed looking approach and briefly explain them.

3. Give four examples of different physical properties of art that one might look at when using a directed looking approach to art appreciation.

4. What are two techniques for creating the illusion of distance?

5. Analyze Lange's photograph *Migrant Mother: Nipomo, California* on page 121 in terms of (a) subject matter, (b) formal elements, and (c) viewer perspective.

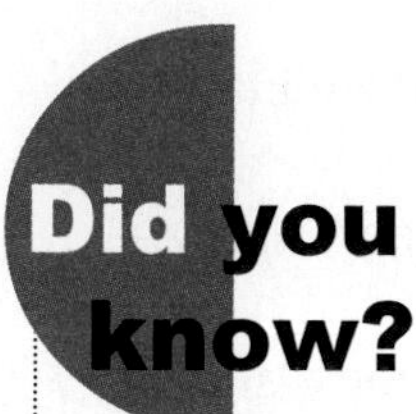

Dorothea Lange was a documentary photographer and photojournalist, best known for work portraying the poor and homeless during the American Depression era (1929-1935).

ACTIVITY 11 COMPARING IDEAS

1. Compare your answers to the preceding questions with a partner or group. If you have different answers, check your notes and discuss your reasons for making your choices.

2. Compare your rewritten notes to the sample rewritten notes in Appendix D. Notice the organization. Is yours similar or different? Are your notes equally effective in making important ideas stand out?

ACTIVITY 12 ACADEMIC WORD LIST VOCABULARY

Match the word to its meaning. Write the correct letter in the space provided. Examples are given to help you see words in context.

Group 1

a. having similarities or connections (between two events)
b. general; as a whole
c. tending to examine critically, breaking things down into causes and effects
d. related to ideas or feelings but not concrete things

___	1. *parallel*	The teacher commented on the parallel course of their lives; both had grown up poor in small towns and moved to cities in 2008 to study.
___	2. *overall*	My overall opinion is that the movie was good, although I have a few criticisms.
___	3. *abstract*	When he spoke, he was too abstract, so I asked for some specific examples.
___	4. *analytical*	Stop being so analytical; just tell me if you liked the movie or not!

Group 2

a. a way of understanding or studying meaning and truth and life
b. a part or aspect
c. the ability to see deeply into something; perception
d. the range; the extent

___	5. *insight*	Good psychiatrists have insight, which helps them understand their patients.
___	6. *philosophy*	His philosophy about parenting involved putting the child's needs first.
___	7. *element*	That movie has all the elements of a "blockbuster" hit: action, big stars, great visuals.
___	8. *scope*	An in-depth discussion is beyond the scope of this short talk.

Group 3

a. way of handling or considering something
b. communication
c. level
d. a part of a whole

___	9. *component*	She hooked up all the components of her music system: the speakers, the CD player, the radio, the receiver.

___ 10. *approach* His approach to cooking was very creative; he often created new combinations.

___ 11. *interaction* There was little interaction between the artist and model; they barely spoke.

___ 12. *layer* There are a lot of layers of meaning in that story.

ACTIVITY 13 USING VOCABULARY

You will hear vocabulary from the lecture, reading, and discussion in different contexts. Listen and check (✓) the letter of the closest paraphrase of the information.

Group A

1. ___ **a.** My friend let me use her new camera.
   ___ **b.** My friend suggested ways to use my new camera.
   ___ **c.** My friend gave me some money to buy a new camera.

2. ___ **a.** My first pictures were very clear.
   ___ **b.** My first pictures weren't very clear.
   ___ **c.** My first pictures were outstanding.

3. ___ **a.** I tried to photograph some people indoors.
   ___ **b.** I tried to photograph a landscape.
   ___ **c.** I tried to photograph some arranged objects.

4. ___ **a.** I wanted to create an illusion of a red rose on a table.
   ___ **b.** I wanted people to immediately notice the red rose.
   ___ **c.** I wanted the red rose to be unrecognizable and blend in with the table.

Group B

1. ___ **a.** My boss told me explicitly that he wasn't happy with my work.
   ___ **b.** My boss suggested indirectly that he wasn't happy with my work.
   ___ **c.** My boss lied to me about my chances for promotion at work.

2. ___ **a.** He never shows anger about things I do.
   ___ **b.** He never shows pleasure in things I do.
   ___ **c.** He never shows interest in things I do.

3. ___ **a.** It's a good thing that I enjoy my role as a parent.
   ___ **b.** It's easy to see that I'm not happy.
   ___ **c.** I can see that no one around here is happy.

(continued on next page)

4. ____ a. I had earlier experiences with him and I should have paid attention to them.

____ b. When we were students together, I shouldn't have trusted him.

____ c. I had a feeling about him when I first met him; I should have paid attention.

VOCABULARY LEARNING STRATEGY

Learn and use some words in semantic (meaning-related) groups.

ACTIVITY 14 RETAINING VOCABULARY

This studio is full of people pursuing creative projects. Look at it for 2 minutes and then close your book. With a classmate, write sentences describing what you remember happening.

Example
A man with a cap was on a ladder on a stage. He was building a set and putting up lighting. He was probably getting ready for some kind of theatrical performance.

ACTIVITY 15 BEYOND THE LECTURE: SPEAKING AND LISTENING

Bring in a copy or slide of a piece of artwork that you like. Give a short presentation about the artwork, talking about the work in terms of the different categories of directed looking.

LISTENING FOR ORGANIZATION (PART 3)

Goals

- Follow three more organizational plans used by lecturers: describing causal relationships, comparing and contrasting, and generalizing and providing evidence
- Understand and follow the cues that signal these organizational plans
- Listen to and take notes on lectures that use these organizational plans
- Practice using notes to answer various test-type questions

In Units 6 and 7, you practiced recognizing and taking notes using six organizational plans. In this unit, you will learn about and practice three more plans.

DISCUSSION

Talking About Our Academic Interests

1. In your major or area of academic interest, what kinds of things are typically compared or contrasted? Discuss one of these comparisons/contrasts that interests you (e.g., film photography versus digital photography, governments around the world, male/female management styles).
2. Give an example of an interesting cause and effect relationship that is typically discussed in your major or area of academic interest (e.g. the causes of poverty; the positive and negative effects of outsourcing; architectural design and its impact on communal life).
3. In your major or area of academic interest, are there any strong disagreements among experts (e.g. in the field of political science, experts disagree about which voting system is the best; in the field of economics, experts disagree about ways to prevent inflation)? Talk about a basic disagreement in your field and how the experts support their views. Which side do you tend to support?

Describing a Causal Relationship

In this case, the lecturer's goal is to describe a relationship in which one event leads to (or could lead to) one or more events; or, conversely, to work backwards and discuss causes of an event that has already occurred.

The lecturer might follow one of these patterns:

- a description of a goal, a problem, or the circumstances surrounding an event
- the causes of, or reasons for, the goal, problem, or circumstances
- the effects of the problem or circumstances
- the solution to a problem
- the means to achieve a goal

Notes from a lecture using this pattern might look like this:

> Earthquakes:
>
> Causes:
>
> –(infrequent) atomic explosions or volcanic eruptions
>
> – (most) slippages along Earth's crust
>
> Effect – releases energy – radiates from source in waves

CUES TO RECOGNIZE DESCRIPTIONS

1. Words and phrases signaling a causal relationship:

   Owing to the fact that …

   Because / Since …

   Conditional sentences: If …, (then) …

   (Now) this is due to …

   It has nothing to do with X, but rather …

   What you need is X … Then Y will happen.

   A major cause of … is …

   One of the fundamental reasons for this is …

2. Words or phrases signaling the effect of a previously stated event:

   Thus, …

   Therefore, …

   Consequently, …

   For these reasons, …

3. Rhetorical questions signaling a discussion of the cause of a previously stated event:

   How can we best understand this?

   What led up to this point?

   Why is this the case?

   Your goal is X. How are you going to do that?

4. Rhetorical questions signaling a discussion of the solution to a previously stated problem:

   What can be done about this?

   Now, what are some possible responses to this?

   How can we solve this?

Exercise 1

You will hear three lecture excerpts that describe causal relationships. First read the information about each excerpt. Then, while listening, take notes in the spaces provided.

Example

Excerpt from a lecture on conflict resolution

Problem	Conflict Resolution:
	Sharif (50 yrs. ago):
	Contact hypothesis: bring people together → resolve conflict
	Didn't work! (just 1st step)
Solution	NEED super-ordinate goal (to work on dependently)

1. Excerpt from a lecture on eight steps of topic analysis for library research

Event	7th Step — See topic in broadest way
	— Think about ac. disciplines related to topic
Reason	Why?

2. Excerpt from a lecture on evolutionary psychology

VOCABULARY

framework: a system for considering something
propagate: to reproduce
genetic material: material relating to genes (the part of a living cell that contains parents' characteristics)

Goal

Means

Goal as organism? ________________

How?

3. Excerpt from a lecture on Asian-Pacific immigration to the United States

Cause

Effect

1965 — U.S. changes imm. law

↓ (previously # of Asians small b/c quota ~ 100 people per country/yr)

B Comparing and Contrasting

A lecturer might choose to show the difference between two things that seem similar by contrasting them, or show similarities between two seemingly different things by comparing them. Often, a lecturer will both compare and contrast.

The lecturer could first talk about each item individually, and then compare and contrast them. Notes from a lecture using this pattern might look like this:

Diff. betw. penguins & most flying birds?

Flying birds:

- long, wide wings
- thin layer, short feathers
- bones: light, hollow (filled w/ air)
- lean over (not stand straight)
- long, thin feet (to sit on branches)

Penguins:

- don't fly
  - Why? bones heavier & more solid than flying birds (so ↑ weight for swim/dive)
- have short, stiff wings ("flippers" to push thru water)
- stand upright
- have thick, webbed feet (wide, strong)
- 2 thick layers feathers (w/ waxy oil so waterproof in H_2O)

BOTH lay eggs, warm-blooded, have wings, feathers, legs, beaks

The lecturer may also compare and/or contrast the items point by point. Notes from a lecture using this pattern might look like this:

	FLYING BIRDS	PENGUINS
Fly?	✓	NO
Bones	Light, hollow (filled w/ air)	Heavier & more solid (so ↑weight for swim/dive)
Wings	Long, wide	Short, stiff ("flippers" so push in H_2O)
Posture	Lean over	Stand upright
Feet	Long, thin (to sit on branches)	Thick, webbed (wide, strong) to walk
Feathers	Thin layer, short	2 thick layers (w/ waxy oil to waterproof)
Lay eggs?	✓	✓
Warmblooded?	✓	✓

For either style, the note-taker should try to visually represent the differences and/or similarities between the items.

In the second set of notes above, it is very easy to glance down the left-hand margin and see the areas of comparison and contrast, instead of just a collection of unrelated similarities and differences. Rather, the similarities and differences are grouped according to topic. This is not always possible when taking notes, but it is very helpful to do when revising or rewriting notes.

CUES TO RECOGNIZE COMPARISONS AND CONTRASTS

1. Words and phrases indicating a contrast between preceding and following information:

   But / However ...
   On the contrary ...
   Conversely, ...
   In contrast, ...
   The critical difference is that...
   In direct opposition, ...
   Now, let's look at the other side.
   In typical development, X happens. Maybe X is not happening here. ...
   The big thing is the debate between X and Y ...
   ... here, the situation is different...

2. Words and phrases indicating a similarity between preceding and following information:

   This is very similar to ...
   Likewise, ...
   Along the same lines, ...
   In the same fashion / manner / way, ...
   There are some striking similarities between ... and ...
   Here too / again, ...

3. Rhetorical questions signaling an explanation of similarities or differences:

   How can we distinguish X and Y?
   What are some ways to tell X from Y?
   What sets these apart?

4. Stress emphasizing items being compared or their distinguishing characteristics:

   Now what about the students who <u>didn't</u> get the extra help as compared to those who <u>did</u> ...

5. Body language suggesting a comparison:

   For example, hands can be used to emphasize different sides of a comparison / contrast.

on the one hand

on the other hand

Exercise 2

You will hear three lecture excerpts that include comparisons and contrasts. Read each excerpt. Then, while listening, take notes in the space provided.

Example

Excerpt from a lecture on biology, in particular autism

VOCABULARY

autism: a mental disorder characterized by difficulty communicating or connecting with others

Brain size in autism: different

Born similar or slightly smaller

In 1st 2nd yr, rapid growth → head/brain larger/heavier

	Typical Develop:
Pruning back not happening?	Brain establish connections
Connectivity diff?	Cut back connections
Noisy system?	Leave USEFUL ones

1. Excerpt from the first day introduction of a psychology class

2. Excerpt from a lecture on human development

VOCABULARY

innate: possessed at birth
predisposition: a tendency; an inclination

Empiricist View | Nativist View

3. Excerpt from a lecture on ecology

VOCABULARY

shrub: a bush, a woody plant

Typical deciduous woodland

Typical coniferous woodland

Rewrite these notes on a separate sheet of paper to emphasize the points of comparison. Consider drawing pictures to help yourself visualize the information. Then compare your rewritten notes with a classmate.

C Recognizing Generalizations and their Support

In this case, the lecturer makes a generalization and provides evidence for it. The generalization can either precede the evidence or follow it. Most often the generalization precedes the evidence. A model might look like the following:

Generalization about intended topic
+
Evidence for the generalization
+
(Optional) Restatement of the generalization

With this pattern, the listener must be especially attentive at the beginning in order to understand the generalization. Once the generalization is understood, the listener can focus on noting the supporting evidence.

In the following lecture notes, the generalization precedes the evidence:

Music benefits health

- Study: Finland, 6 mo. study, 60 recent stroke victims
- Findings: exposure to music, at least 1 hr/day → ↑ verbal mem by 60% compared to 18% improvement w/ audiobooks

Caution: Music alone not miracle cure!

The generalization can also follow the evidence. This happens when the lecturer leads the audience to a generalization that is presented at the end as a conclusion. A model might look like the following:

Statement of intended topic
+
Evidence in form of anecdote(s), observation(s), test description(s), narrative(s), and/or factual detail(s) regarding topic
+
Generalization (conclusion) based on evidence

With this pattern, the listener must follow the speaker's train of thought and be especially attentive to the final conclusions.

In the following lecture notes, the generalization follows the evidence:

Effects of meditation on brain?

—study of 20 experienced meditators-------------------- 15 nonmeditators

– did brain scan—told to meditate | told "RELAX"

– found ↑ thickness in parts of brain related to attention & processing sensory input

∴ Meditation can change adult brain physically.

(similar to study of musicians: ↑ thickness in music-assoc. areas of brain)

CUES TO RECOGNIZE A GENERALIZATION AND EVIDENCE

1. Words or phrases signaling a generalization or conclusion:

   Thus, ...
   Therefore, ...
   In conclusion, ...
   (So), to conclude, ...
   Research has demonstrated (proven / shown) that ...

2. Phrases referring to previous evidence and signaling a conclusion:

   The logical conclusion to draw (to be drawn) from this is ...
   What this clearly shows us is that...
   From this evidence, we can (predict / infer) that...
   All of these factors add up to ...
   They did this study and what they found is ...

3. Phrases or sentences signaling evidence or support for a generalization:

   This has been shown (proven / demonstrated) by ...
   There is extensive evidence that X happens (and I will show you that in a couple of minutes)
   Statistics (Research / Data / Studies / Evidence) show(s) ...

4. Rhetorical questions signaling evidence:

   How do we know this is true?
   What leads us to believe this is the case?

5. Rhetorical questions signaling a generalization:

   What (conclusions can we draw / lessons can we learn) from this?
   What does this tell (demonstrate / show) us?

Exercise 3

You will hear three lecture excerpts containing generalizations and evidence. First read the information. Then, while listening, take notes in the space provided.

Example

Excerpt from a lecture on psychology

VOCABULARY

placebo: substance that looks like real medicine but contains no drugs; typically used for comparison when testing new drugs

vomit: to throw up; to expel (food from the stomach) through the mouth

Generalization	"Placebo effect" shows POWER of MIND
Evidence	Research by Herbert Benson:
	1) pregnant ♀ w/ stomach problems; dr. gave placebo; said would stop vomiting-------- they got better!
	2) pregnant ♀ w/ same prob.; dr. gave ipecac (drug to cause vomiting); dr. said it would make them STOP vomiting -------- vomiting stopped!
Generalization	Medicine (esp. West.) IGNORES power of mind
(conclusion)	Medicine important, BUT sometimes MIND MORE imp.

1. Excerpt from a lecture on memory-improving drugs

VOCABULARY

maze: an enclosed system with many confusing pathways

Generalization	
Evidence	

(continued on next page)

2. Excerpt from a lecture on Asian-Pacific immigration to the United States

VOCABULARY

heterogeneous: consisting of different kinds
dialect: a regional variety of a language

Generalization

Evidence

3. Excerpt from a lecture on zoology

VOCABULARY

orangutan / "orang," chimpanzees: animals in the ape family
ambiguous: able to be understood in two different ways

Evidence

Do animals have a sense of self? If see reflection, do they know WHO?

–Charles Darwin study:
- –to London Zoo, put mirror to cage of 2 orangs
- –orangs looked, made faces BUT behavior/thought ambiguous

–Gordon Gallop 1970s study: MORE FORMAL test
- – showed chimps reflection many days
- – anesthetized chimps & put 2 red marks on face (not felt/smelled)
- – What happened when woke?
- – TOUCHED marks; then used mirror to see more

Generalization

∴

LECTURE 9

Hall's Classification of Cultures (Sociology)

Vocabulary

Related to International Travel and Relations

Check (✓) the words you know. Underline the words you want to learn. Then check their meaning with your instructor or in a dictionary.

embassy
consulate
ministry of ...

ambassador
diplomat
consul
minister of ...

diplomacy
negotiation
treaty

protocol
etiquette

visa
passport
customs

currency
exchange rate

tourism
ecotourism

ACTIVITY 1 PRE-LECTURE DISCUSSION

This lecture is about the views of Dr. Edward Hall, an anthropologist who specialized in intercultural relations. Some of his work focused on the different assumptions that people have toward time, space, and other people.

1. Circle the number that corresponds to your feelings about each statement.

   1 = disagree strongly
   2 = disagree somewhat
   3 = neither agree nor disagree
   4 = agree somewhat
   5 = agree strongly

   a. I get impatient when someone is late. 1 2 3 4 5

   b. I am rarely late. 1 2 3 4 5

   c. I would be insulted if someone was supposed to meet me at 10:00 and arrived at 10:15 and didn't apologize or give me a good excuse. 1 2 3 4 5

   d. If I have a party and invite people for 7:00, I expect them to really show up at 7:00, not 7:30. 1 2 3 4 5

(continued on next page)

e. I believe in the expression "Time is money." 1 2 3 4 5

f. I get upset when I feel as if I'm wasting time. 1 2 3 4 5

g. I always wear a wristwatch. 1 2 3 4 5

h. I try to do as much as possible in one day and I get frustrated if something (e.g., traffic) prevents me from doing what I want. 1 2 3 4 5

Calculate your score. What does it tell you about your attitude toward time? Are there any great variations in scores in the class? Do you think any of the variations are due to cultural attitudes?

2. Circle the number that corresponds to your feelings about interpersonal relationships.

   a. If I enter into a verbal contract with someone, I always keep my word. 1 2 3 4 5

   b. If someone enters into a verbal contract with me, I trust them and do not feel it is necessary to get it all on paper. 1 2 3 4 5

   c. I would not marry a person who came from a disreputable family. 1 2 3 4 5

   d. I would never do something that would shame my family, even if I believed it was right. 1 2 3 4 5

   e. If there is corruption in a company, I believe that the head of that company should take responsibility, even if she or he is not involved. 1 2 3 4 5

   f. In decisions involving what is best for me as an individual versus what is best for my family as a whole, I will always decide on the side of my family. 1 2 3 4 5

   Calculate your score. What does it tell you about your attitude toward interpersonal relationships? Are there any great variations in scores in the class? Are any of the variations due to cultural attitudes?

3. What do the following two statements mean? Do you agree or disagree? Why?

   a. All human beings are captives of their culture.

   b. What we think of as mind is really internalized culture.

ACTIVITY 2 PREPARING FOR THE LECTURE

The title of the lecture is "Hall's Classification of Cultures." What do you expect the lecturer to say about classifying cultures? Brainstorm ideas with your classmates.

Listen to the introduction and answer the following questions.

1. The lecturer said, "It's possible that people from different cultures have different, unconscious, ingrained assumptions about the world regarding such important and basic ideas as interpersonal relationships, time, personal space." What does it mean if an assumption or belief is "unconscious" and "ingrained"?

2. Check (✓) the items that are true about Edward Hall:

   ___ **a.** He is an anthropologist.

   ___ **b.** He is an American Indian.

   ___ **c.** He studied American Indians.

   ___ **d.** He is interested in how cultures interact.

3. The lecturer said that Hall believes that cultures can be classified along a continuum, ranging from "high context" to "low context." What will the lecturer probably do in the remainder of the lecture? Check (✓) as many as are appropriate.

   ___ **a.** define these terms

   ___ **b.** compare and contrast these types of cultures

   ___ **c.** give examples of these types of cultures

   ___ **d.** judge which cultures are best

   ___ **e.** discuss how each of these types of cultures handles time

   ___ **f.** discuss how each of these types of cultures handles personal space

   ___ **g.** discuss how each of these types of cultures handles relationships

   ___ **h.** discuss the importance of travel

   ___ **i.** discuss the pleasures of travel

Vocabulary

Useful International Acronyms

Check (✓) the acronyms you know. Underline the words you want to learn.

UN: United Nations
NATO: North Atlantic Treaty Organization
EEU: European Economic Union
NAFTA: North Atlantic Free Trade Association
ASEAN: Association of Southeast Asian Nations
AFTA: ASEAN Free Trade Area
WTO: World Trade Organization
IMF: International Monetary Fund
OAU: Organization of African Unity
OPEC: Organization of Petroleum Exporting Countries
WHO : World Health Organization

ACTIVITY 3 LISTENING FOR THE LARGER PICTURE

Listen to the lecture once without taking notes. Then, fill in the blanks in the summary and discuss your responses to the questions below.

1. The goal of this lecture is to make the audience aware of Hall's classification of cultures on a continuum from ____________ (1.) to ____________ (2.). In order to understand this classification, the lecturer defines certain terms and gives examples of how each type of culture would react in situations involving ____________ (3.), ____________ (4.), and ____________ (5.).

2. a. Explain the terms *high-context culture* and *low-context culture*.

   b. Reread the statements about time and interpersonal relationships on pages 143-144. How do you think a person from a high-context culture would respond to them? a person from a low-context culture?

ACTIVITY 4 ORGANIZATION

Read this summary of the lecture organization.

In order to present this classification of cultures, the lecturer defines each type of culture and gives examples of how it functions in real life. These examples are further classified in terms of time, space, and personal relationships. The lecture organization can be outlined as follows:

I. Introduction

II. High-context cultures

- A. Definition
- B. Examples regarding interpersonal relationships
- C. Examples regarding attitudes toward time
- D. Examples regarding attitudes toward personal space

III. Low-context cultures

- A. Definition
- B. Examples regarding interpersonal relationships
- C. Examples regarding attitudes toward time
- D. Examples regarding attitudes toward personal space

IV. Conclusion

This lecture can also be seen as having a comparison and contrast pattern, because the two items are discussed to differentiate them from each other.

Do you remember any of the examples the lecturer gave to show attitudes about interpersonal relationships, time, or space? Discuss with a partner.

ACTIVITY 5 DEFINING VOCABULARY

The following words and expressions were used in the lecture. You may remember the contexts in which you heard them. Listen to another example of each word or expression in a new context. Check (✓) the letter of the definition that most closely matches what you think the word or expression means.

1. ***assumption****

    ___ **a.** a lie that is told to deceive another person

    ___ **b.** a mistake that is made on purpose

    ___ **c.** a conclusion that is reached without proof or demonstration

2. ***entity****

    ___ **a.** an event that takes place indoors

    ___ **b.** something that exists as a particular and separate unit

    ___ **c.** an event that takes place outdoors, in natural surroundings

3. ***negotiation***

    ___ **a.** a demand presented to get what one wants

    ___ **b.** a discussion that occurs to reach an agreement

    ___ **c.** a workers' organization

4. ***commodity****

    ___ **a.** something useful that can be traded, sold, or saved

    ___ **b.** something immaterial; something that is not concrete

    ___ **c.** a group of individuals who interact with each other

5. ***restrain****

    ___ **a.** to try too hard

    ___ **b.** to control; to limit behavior

    ___ **c.** to give someone a prison sentence

6. ***feel violated****

    ___ **a.** to feel that one's rights and wishes have been ignored

    ___ **b.** to feel angry and want to harm others

    ___ **c.** to feel close to another person and want to help him or her

7. ***reform***

    ___ **a.** a harsher, more severe punishment

    ___ **b.** the destruction or elimination of a building

    ___ **c.** a correction of an injustice

(continued on next page)

8. *rigid**

___ a. inflexible; not easily changed

___ b. flexible; easily changed

___ c. extremely cold; below freezing

The following idioms and sayings reflect attitudes toward time, space, and interpersonal relationships. Listen and then check (✓) the letter of the definition that most closely explains the idiom or saying.

9. *shoulder the blame*

___ a. to blame another person for an action

___ b. to take responsibility for an action

___ c. to shift responsibility for an action to another person

10. *take for granted*

___ a. to appreciate and value something fully when it is offered

___ b. to leave a bad situation in the hopes of finding something better

___ c. to consider, use, or accept without appreciating the value

11. *Her word is her bond.*

___ a. She repeatedly lies.

___ b. She does what she promises.

___ c. She can't stop talking.

12. *pass the buck*

___ a. to send money to another person

___ b. to shift responsibility to another person

___ c. to accept responsibility for someone's debts

13. *The buck stops here.*

___ a. I will take your money.

___ b. I will accept responsibility.

___ c. I will shift responsibility to someone else.

14. *Time is money.*

___ a. Time can be viewed in terms of money lost, earned, or wasted.

___ b. Money can help you live longer (e.g., buy better medical care).

___ c. Money can buy happy times (e.g., parties).

ACTIVITY 6 LISTENING AND NOTE-TAKING

Listen to the lecture a second time. Take notes using the following format, but use your own paper and allow more space.

Introduction	
Cultures: type 1 definition	High-context cultures
Examples re: interpersonal relationships	
Examples re: personal space	
Examples re: time	
Disadvantages	
Advantages	
Cultures: type 2 definition	Low-context cultures
Examples re: interpersonal relationships	
Examples re: personal space	
Examples re: time	
Disadvantages	
Advantages	
Conclusions	Low-context ——— High-context Ger./Swiss Ger. Scand. U.S. Fren. Eng. Ital. Span. Greek Arab

ACTIVITY 7 REPLAY QUESTION

One word that indicates a contrast is "whereas." Listen to how the word is used in this section of the lecture and note the contrast it makes.

low-context culture: ____________________

high-context culture: ____________________

LISTENING AND NOTE-TAKING STRATEGIES

1. Review your notes as soon as possible after listening, adding information that you remember but didn't have time to note.
2. Ask classmates for specific pieces of information that you might have missed.
3. Consider rewriting your notes soon after listening to make the relationship between ideas more clear. Make sure comparison/contrasts, important generalizations, and cause/effect relationships are immediately apparent.

ACTIVITY 8 "OTHER VOICES" FOLLOW-UP

A student goes to his professor's office. Listen to their conversation and answer the questions below.

1. What does the student say he wants the professor to do? Check (✓) one.
   ___ **a.** let him do something for extra credit
   ___ **b.** change his midterm grade
   ___ **c.** recalculate his average
   ___ **d.** give him advice on what to study for the final exam

2. Which is NOT true about the professor? Check (✓) one.
   ___ **a.** She met with the student after the midterm and gave suggestions for improving his grade.
   ___ **b.** She doesn't give extra credit assignments at the last minute.
   ___ **c.** She wrote her grading policy in the class syllabus.
   ___ **d.** She believes the student can pass the class if he studies for the final exam.

3. How was the teacher's attitude during the conversation? Check (✓) one.
   ___ **a.** She started out annoyed and then got more patient and sympathetic.
   ___ **b.** She started out patient and sympathetic and then got annoyed.
   ___ **c.** She was sympathetic and patient throughout.
   ___ **d.** She was annoyed throughout.

4. The professor said, "A rule is a rule," "I stand by my rules," "It's all clearly spelled out in the syllabus," and "The time for that has come and gone." Does she demonstrate more of a high- or low-context culture viewpoint? Why?

____

____

____

5. Discuss the following question in small groups:
The student, at times, seems to be trying to "negotiate" with the professor. Would this be usual or unusual behavior in your native culture? What advice, if any, would you give this student and professor?

ACTIVITY 9 POST-LECTURE READING AND DISCUSSION

Read the international business scenario described below by an Indian business executive, Kurien Joseph. Then discuss the questions on the next page in small groups.

I remember visiting the newly independent nation of Turkmenistan in 1992. At the first meeting, in Askhabad, I was received by a team of six or seven executives at 10 A.M. My next appointment was at 11:30 A.M.

This meeting started off with a long speech, with intermittent[1] translations by my interpreter about how wonderful they felt to receive me, an Indian, from the country of Babar, Humayun,[2] and so on. After more than ten minutes of these obviously heartfelt sentiments,[3] I got a chance to respond.

In about a minute or so I reciprocated[4] their sentiments and then, in typical business style, introduced my company, my product range, the advantages of doing business with us, and so on. I finished my spiel[5] in about ten minutes.

Then it was their turn again. This time, each of the remaining five or six executives spoke. As I learned later, each of them was the head of a particular department and therefore had something specific to discuss. I had my notebook open and my pen ready to pick up any business possibilities. To my utter[6] surprise, and even irritation at that time, each of these executives went into a long speech, welcoming me and speaking about Timur,[7] Samarkand,[8] Babar. It went on till 11:20 A.M.

And then, mercifully,[9] the speeches stopped. I was cordially[10] and quite ceremoniously invited for dinner that evening. "What about our business discussions?" I whispered to my interpreter, in great disappointment. "Oh, that will be tomorrow," he whispered back..

[1] ***intermittent:*** not continuous
[2] ***Babar*** (1483–1530) founded the Mughal Empire of India. His son, ***Humayun***, was the second Mughal Emperor.
[3] ***sentiments:*** feelings
[4] ***reciprocate:*** to give something equal back in exchange
[5] ***spiel:*** (informal) a story (usually told to convince someone)
[6] ***utter:*** complete; total
[7] ***Timur*** (1336–1405) conquered lands throughout Asia, including India and Turkmenistan
[8] ***Samarkand***, one of the oldest existing cities in the world, is in Uzbekistan and was the capital of Timur's empire
[9] ***merciful:*** showing kindness
[10] ***cordial:*** polite

1. a. Apply Hall's theories to the scenario on page 151. How might culturally different expectations explain the different actions and perspectives of the executives from Turkmenistan and India?

   b. The Indian business executive also worked in Australia for four years. Would you consider his behavior and attitudes to be closer to the low-context or the high-context end of the continuum? What about the business executives from Turkmenistan?

2. How does Hall's classification system fit when you apply it to your own culture or what you know of other cultures? If your culture was not on the continuum, where would you place it?

3. Do you think that Hall's classification system is valid? Do you see any problems with it? If so, what are they?

ACTIVITY 10 USING YOUR NOTES

Use your notes to answer the questions on a separate sheet of paper.

1. How does Hall define high-context and low-context culture?

2. True or False?

   ___ a. Hall believes that cultures are either high-context or low-context.

   ___ b. Hall believes that most people are aware of their culture's assumptions about time, space, and interpersonal relations.

   ___ c. A culture in which who you know is more important than what you know is a low-context culture.

   ___ d. "Business negotiations took place and the participants simply shook hands to finalize the deal." This would be reasonable in a low-context culture.

   ___ e. Hall would predict that, generally, members of low-context cultures would not break the law because they would not want to bring disgrace to their families.

   ___ f. A culture that values individuality is a high-context culture.

   ___ g. Hall would predict that people in low-context cultures would prefer that visitors call before dropping by to visit.

3. Define each view of time and give one example of how it could affect one's acts and attitudes in everyday life: (a) polychronic view of time and (b) monochronic view of time.

4. According to Hall, what are the advantages and disadvantages of (a) a high-context culture and (b) a low-context culture?

5. Give four examples of how Hall's ideas could have relevance for international business negotiations.

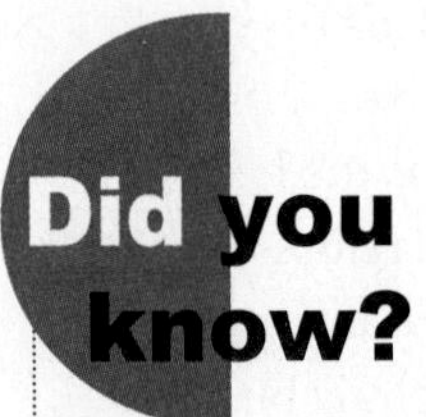

William Shakespeare (1564-1616), British poet and playwright, said, "Better three hours too soon than a minute too late."

ACTIVITY 11 COMPARING IDEAS

1. Compare your answers with a partner or group. If you have different answers, check your notes and discuss your reasons for making your choices.

2. Compare your rewritten notes to the sample rewritten notes in Appendix D. Notice the organization. Is yours similar or different? Are your notes equally effective in making important ideas stand out?

ACTIVITY 12 ACADEMIC WORD LIST VOCABULARY

Match the word and its meaning. Write the correct letter in the space provided. Examples are given to help you see words in context.

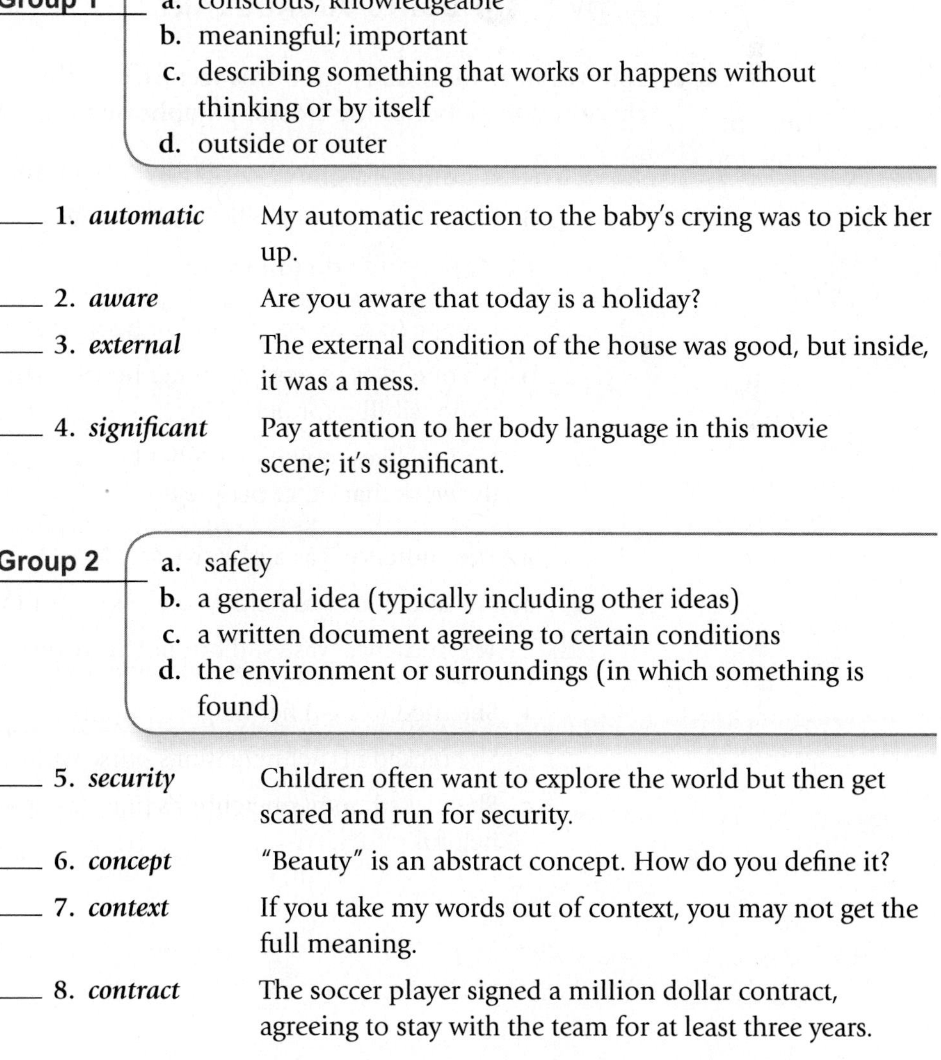

Group 1

a. conscious; knowledgeable
b. meaningful; important
c. describing something that works or happens without thinking or by itself
d. outside or outer

___	1. *automatic*	My automatic reaction to the baby's crying was to pick her up.
___	2. *aware*	Are you aware that today is a holiday?
___	3. *external*	The external condition of the house was good, but inside, it was a mess.
___	4. *significant*	Pay attention to her body language in this movie scene; it's significant.

Group 2

a. safety
b. a general idea (typically including other ideas)
c. a written document agreeing to certain conditions
d. the environment or surroundings (in which something is found)

___	5. *security*	Children often want to explore the world but then get scared and run for security.
___	6. *concept*	"Beauty" is an abstract concept. How do you define it?
___	7. *context*	If you take my words out of context, you may not get the full meaning.
___	8. *contract*	The soccer player signed a million dollar contract, agreeing to stay with the team for at least three years.

(continued on next page)

Group 3

a. to strengthen
b. to give or allow (what is asked for)
c. to keep (thoughts, feelings) inside
d. to place a burden, weight, or demand on

___	9. *impose*	The government imposed an additional tax on consumer products, raising prices.
___	10. *grant*	Her employer granted her request for three days of vacation in June.
___	11. *internalize*	It is unhealthy to internalize all your feelings; you need to share them.
___	12. *reinforce*	The teacher repeated the idea in order to reinforce the lesson.

ACTIVITY 13 USING VOCABULARY

You will hear vocabulary from this lecture in different contexts. Listen and check (✓) the letter of the closest paraphrase of the information.

1. ___ a. He won't accept responsibility when things go wrong.
   ___ b. He accepts responsibility when things go wrong.
   ___ c. He refuses to do extra work.

2. ___ a. No one likes to work with her because she steals money.
   ___ b. No one likes to work with her because she never accepts responsibility for her actions.
   ___ c. No one likes to work with her because she always wants credit for the work that other people do.

3. ___ a. The audience was aggressive and loud.
   ___ b. The audience was neither aggressive nor loud.
   ___ c. The audience was loud but not aggressive.

4. ___ a. She tried to steal her neighbor's purse.
   ___ b. She picked up her neighbor's purse without being aware of doing it.
   ___ c. She picked up her neighbor's purse because she wanted to be helpful.

5. ___ **a.** People have flexible expectations about sex roles, and they can easily change these expectations because they were learned later in life.

___ **b.** People have inflexible and deeply felt expectations about sex roles because they were learned early in life.

___ **c.** People have deeply felt expectations about sex roles. However, these feelings can change.

6. ___ **a.** She doesn't need privacy and loves it when people visit without calling first.

___ **b.** She feels that her privacy is not respected when people visit without calling first.

___ **c.** She has been quite upset by visitors who arrived unexpectedly.

7. ___ **a.** The voters wanted changes in the education system.

___ **b.** The voters wanted a completely new education system.

___ **c.** The voters wanted the leaders to create an education system.

8. ___ **a.** Knowledge and information refer to the same thing.

___ **b.** Knowledge and information refer to two different things.

___ **c.** Knowledge and information are difficult to obtain.

9. ___ **a.** The researcher rated the participants either "happy" or "sad."

___ **b.** The researcher rated the participants "happy," "sad," or "somewhere in between."

___ **c.** The researcher asked the participants to evaluate their own happiness level.

ACTIVITY 14 RETAINING VOCABULARY

VOCABULARY LEARNING STRATEGY

A *collocation* is the relationship between two words or groups of words that often go together and form a common expression. If we hear, read, or practice the words together, the words become "glued" together in our minds. Try learning some word collocations.

Consider some collocations with the verbs "commit" and "grant" on the next page.

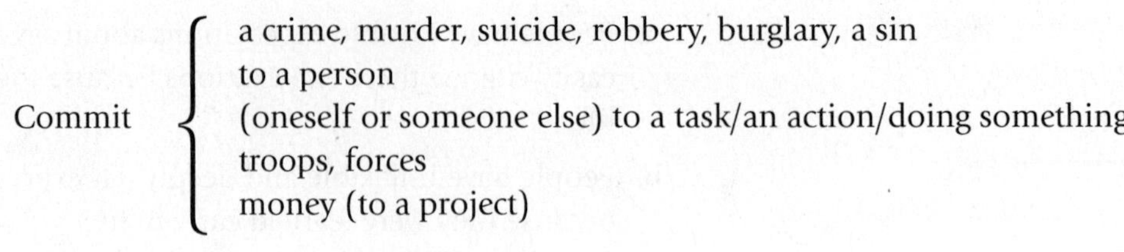

Commit
- a crime, murder, suicide, robbery, burglary, a sin
- to a person
- (oneself or someone else) to a task/an action/doing something
- troops, forces
- money (to a project)

Grant (someone)
- a wish, a request
- permission
- rights
- authority
- leave
- access
- benefits

Discuss these questions with a group. Use some of the collocations listed above.

1. Have you ever witnessed someone committing a crime?
2. Have you ever committed yourself to a project that ended up being harder than you expected? What happened?
3. What should you consider before committing yourself to another person?
4. If you were the president, where would you commit troops, if anywhere?
5. If you were a world leader, would you commit millions of dollars to space exploration? Why or why not?
6. If someone granted you three wishes, what would you wish for?
7. If someone granted you the authority to change the school system, what would you change?
8. If someone granted you access to any leader, whom would you want to meet with?
9. If someone granted you 3 weeks leave from your work or educational responsibilities, what would you do with your time?
10. Should 18-year-olds be granted the right to vote?

ACTIVITY 15 BEYOND THE LECTURE: WRITING

Hall's work focuses on cross-cultural differences relating to time, space, and interpersonal relationships. Write about a specific event from your cross-cultural experience that relates to one or more of these categories.

LECTURE 10

Earthquakes: Can They Be Predicted? (Geology)

Vocabulary

Related to Earthquakes

Check (✓) the words you know. Underline the words you want to learn. Then check their meaning with your instructor or in a dictionary.

earthquake/quake
temblor
tremor
aftershock
foreshock

tsunami
tidal wave

to shake
to vibrate
seismic wave
seismic activity

Richter scale
earthquake magnitude

epicenter
fault (line/zone)
tectonic plate
the earth's crust

seismologist
seismology

destruction, to destroy
devastation, to devastate
collapse, to collapse

earthquake preparedness

ACTIVITY 1 PRE-LECTURE READING AND DISCUSSION

Discuss the following in small groups.

1. Read the following excerpt from a newspaper science column. Then answer the questions that follow.

Q: What site on Earth has the most earthquakes?

A: According to Craig Brunstein of the United States Geological Survey in Denver, no single site qualifies for the honor. Rather, the highest number of earthquakes occur all around the rim of the Pacific Ocean in the so-called ring of fire, where the movement of tectonic plates[1] is the greatest. That ring includes all of the west coast of North and South America, Japan, the Philippines, Indonesia, New Guinea, and New Zealand. This area has not only the largest number of quakes but also the most severe ones.

What do you already know about earthquakes? What do you know about tectonic plates? Brainstorm with your class about the causes and locations of earthquakes.

[1] A dozen or so *plates* make up the surface of the Earth. Their motion is studied in the field of ***plate tectonics***.

2. Read the excerpt below. Then answer the questions that follow.

Warning from Space?

A Russian Scientist Claims He Has Devised[1] a System for Detecting[2] Earthquakes from Outer Space Several Hours before They Hit. U.S. Experts Remain Doubtful

Richard C. Paddock and Robert Lee Hotz, *Los Angeles Times*

Moscow—A Russian scientist says he has come up with a way to predict earthquakes from outer space that could provide a warning as much as three hours in advance of major quakes. The method of forecasting proposed by physics professor Arkady Galper is based on the discovery that electromagnetic waves emanating[3] from Earth just before a big temblor[4] appear to change the behavior of particles[5] in the radiation belt that rings the planet.

Galper, director of the Institute of Space Physics at the Moscow Engineering and Physics Institute, said …

[1] ***devise:*** to create, invent
[2] ***detect:*** to notice
[3] ***emanate:*** to radiate; to come from
[4] ***temblor:*** earthquake
[5] ***particle:*** very small piece; (physics) an extremely small piece of matter

According to the article, what does Galper believe he has discovered? What are the reactions of some in the scientific community? Have you heard of any other techniques for earthquake prediction?

ACTIVITY 2 PREPARING FOR THE LECTURE

The title of the lecture is "Earthquakes: Can They Be Predicted?" How do you expect the lecturer to answer this question? What do you expect the lecturer to talk about? Brainstorm ideas with your classmates.

Listen to the beginning of the lecture.

What do you expect the lecturer to do in the remainder of the lecture? Check (✓) one or more.

____ **a.** talk about what typically causes earthquakes
____ **b.** talk about earthquake-prediction possibilities
____ **c.** give a scientific definition of "earthquakes"
____ **d.** talk about earthquakes caused by atomic explosions
____ **e.** talk about earthquakes caused by volcanic eruptions

ACTIVITY 3 LISTENING FOR THE LARGER PICTURE

Listen to the lecture once without taking notes. Refer to the diagrams on this page as the lecturer talks.

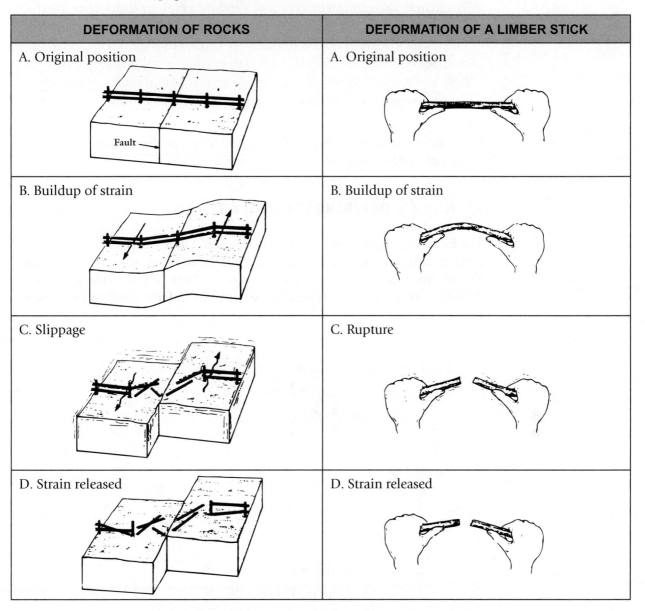

DEFORMATION OF ROCKS	DEFORMATION OF A LIMBER STICK
A. Original position 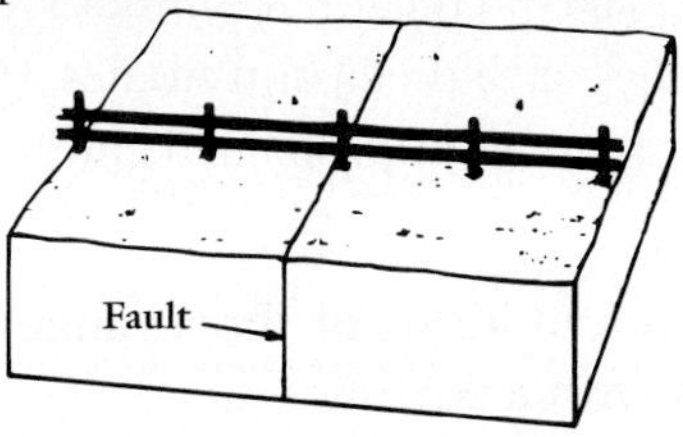 Fault	A. Original position 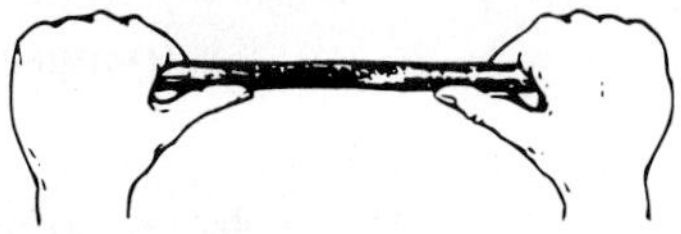
B. Buildup of strain 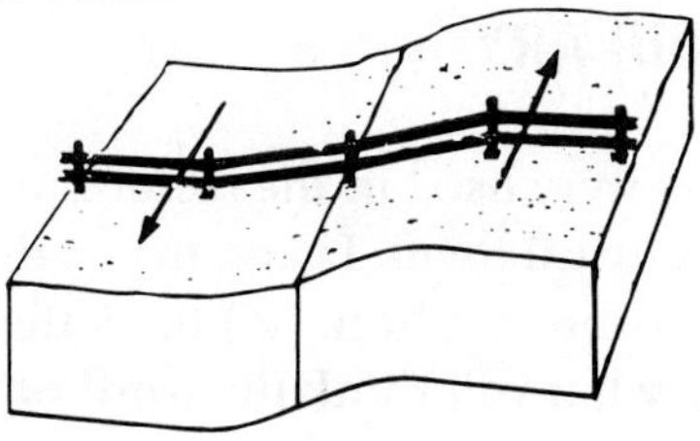	B. Buildup of strain 
C. Slippage 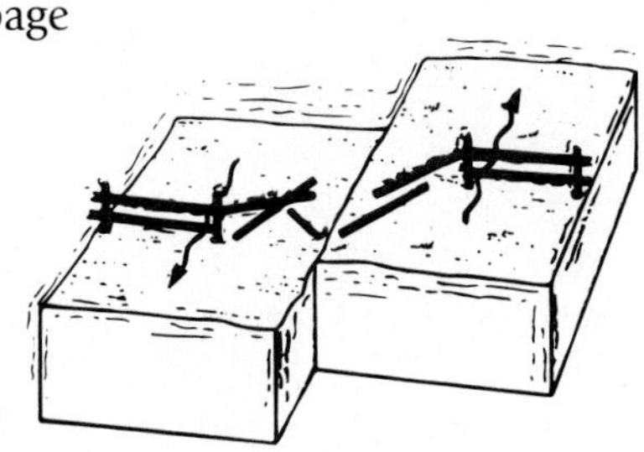	C. Rupture 
D. Strain released 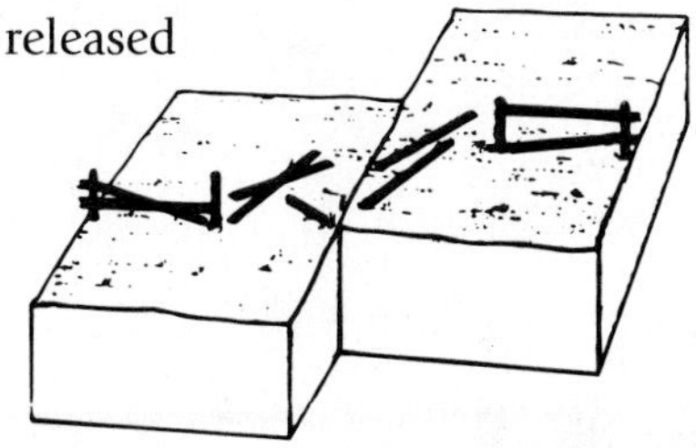	D. Strain released 

After listening, work in small groups to answer the following questions.

1. Look at the diagrams again. Then use your own words to explain what the images demonstrate.
2. What two kinds of earthquake prediction techniques are discussed?
3. What conclusions does the lecturer reach about earthquake prediction?

ACTIVITY 4 ORGANIZATION

Read this summary of the lecture organization.

The lecturer defines the term *earthquakes* and then explains their causes. Then he explains the process of stress buildup and stress release, partly by comparing the process to familiar objects such as bent wooden sticks or rubber bands. He next describes different types of earthquake-prediction techniques that have been investigated—short-range and long-range prediction studies. He uses these studies to make some generalizations about earthquake prediction.

What do you remember about the different kinds of short-range and long-range prediction techniques? Discuss with a partner.

ACTIVITY 5 DEFINING VOCABULARY

The following words and expressions were used in the lecture. You may remember the contexts in which you heard them. Listen to another example of each word or expression in a new context. Check (✓) the letter of the definition that most closely matches what you think the word or expression means.

1. *source**

   ___ a. money; financial resources

   ___ b. liquid poured over food

   ___ c. origin; root; beginning

2. *rapid*

   ___ a. fast

   ___ b. intelligent

   ___ c. careful

3. *radiate*

   ___ a. to do physical work outdoors

   ___ b. to do the same work repeatedly

   ___ c. to send out light or heat

4. *deform*

   ___ a. to spoil the form or appearance of

   ___ b. to form something repeatedly

   ___ c. to create different forms of music

5. *exceed**

___ a. to be less than

___ b. to be equal to

___ c. to be greater than

6. *peculiar*

___ a. dangerous; violent

___ b. unusual; strange

___ c. friendly; helpful

7. *emit*

___ a. to send out; to release

___ b. to paint

___ c. to allow air to enter

8. *foretell*

___ a. to repeat or tell secret information to others

___ b. to have economic problems

___ c. to tell what will happen in the future

9. *evacuate*

___ a. to destroy a building or other structure

___ b. to successfully fight a spreading fire

___ c. to leave or make people leave a threatened place

10. *skeptical*

___ a. excited; pleased and hopeful

___ b. doubting; distrusting

___ c. trusting; willing to believe

11. *cyclical**

___ a. happening in a regular repeated order

___ b. related to technology and scientific research

___ c. related to wheeled vehicles (e.g., motorcycles, bicycles)

12. *interval*

___ a. a medical checkup

___ b. a break or vacation from work

___ c. a period of time between events

ACTIVITY 6 LISTENING AND NOTE-TAKING

Listen to the lecture a second time. Take notes using the following format, but use your own paper and allow more space.

Introduction	Earthquake:
Definition	
Causes	Causes of quakes?
Description of plate tectonics and elastic rebound process	
Research on quake prediction	EQ prediction 2 types quake prediction:
1st type of prediction strategy	short-range pred:
2nd type of prediction strategy	long-range pred:
Conclusions	

ACTIVITY 7 REPLAY QUESTION

Listen to this section from the lecture and answer the question.

Why does the lecturer talk about a pond? Check (✓) one.

____ **a.** To give an example to show what an underwater earthquake might look like

____ **b.** To compare damage caused by a tidal wave to damage caused by earthquakes

____ **c.** To give an analogy to show how energy radiates in waves from an impact

____ **d.** To digress and remember a pond that appeared after an earthquake

ACTIVITY 8 "OTHER VOICES" FOLLOW-UP

Breaking news—an earthquake near Los Angeles! An earthquake specialist, Dr. Kim Hurston, is holding a press conference reporting on the quake.

1. Listen to the specialist and fill in the information about the quake.

What time did it occur?	
What magnitude[1] was the main earthquake?	
How many aftershocks[2] were reported?	
How deep was the main earthquake?	
What are some results of the earthquake?	

LISTENING AND NOTE-TAKING STRATEGIES

1. Review your notes soon after listening, adding information that you remember.
2. Ask classmates for specific pieces of information that you might have missed.
3. Consider rewriting your notes soon after listening to make the relationship between ideas more clear. Make sure comparisons/contrasts, important generalizations, and cause/effect relationships are immediately apparent. Use diagrams or pictures, instead of words, when helpful.

[1] *magnitude:* size
[2] *aftershocks:* smaller earthquakes after a larger one

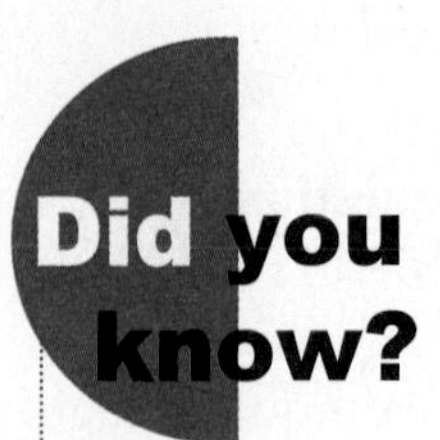

It is estimated that there are 500,000 detectable earthquakes in the world each year. 100,000 of those can be felt, and 100 of them cause damage.

2. Listen to the remainder of the press conference. Reporters asked four questions:
   - How long was the earthquake?
   - People used different words to describe their impression of the earthquake. Some said it was a "rolling motion" and others described it as "jolting." How do you explain the differences in how people perceived the earthquake?
   - What is the chance of this earthquake being a precursor to a larger earthquake?
   - Was there any warning of this earthquake?

   In small groups, write what you remember of Dr. Hurston's answers to each of these questions. Then listen again to check your understanding.

ACTIVITY 9 POST-LECTURE READING AND DISCUSSION

Read the remainder of the article that you started on page 158. Then, work in small groups to answer the questions that follow.

Warning from Space?

A Russian Scientist Claims He Has Devised a System for Detecting Earthquakes from Outer Space Several Hours before They Hit. U.S. Experts Remain Doubtful

Richard C. Paddock and Robert Lee Hotz, *Los Angeles Times*

Moscow—A Russian scientist says he has come up with a way to predict earthquakes from outer space that could provide a warning as much as three hours in advance of major quakes. The method of forecasting proposed by physics professor Arkady Galper is based on the discovery that electromagnetic waves emanating from Earth just before a big temblor appear to change the behavior of particles in the radiation belt that rings the planet.

Galper, director of the Institute of Space Physics at the Moscow Engineering and Physics Institute, said three groups of Russian scientists have corroborated[1] his results. But no major scientific papers have been published on his earthquake forecasting idea and it has not been subjected to the scrutiny[2] of peer review[3] that is standard in the United States.

Indeed, several U.S. earthquake experts queried[4] about Galper's work were deeply skeptical, saying that there was little evidence to support it or any other prediction theory.

Although many researchers over the years have proposed

[1] *corroborate:* to verify the truth of something someone else says

[2] *scrutiny:* close examination

[3] *peer review:* a process of evaluation done by colleagues in the field

[4] *query:* to question

various techniques to predict earthquakes, none have worked in practice. "Most scientists would say that earthquake prediction is a very long way off, if not impossible," said Thomas Henyey, director of the Southern California Earthquake Center.

Henyey called the Russian prediction theory "implausible."[5] To take it seriously, Henyey said, "I would have to see a very, very, careful discussion of the physics of the entire process. You have to be skeptical as to whether some theoretical physicist is stringing together phenomena[6] that may seem plausible but that are extremely unlikely to ever happen in nature. You would also want to see that there have been multiple successes, and one would have to look at that very carefully, too."

Galper acknowledged that, so far, his method of prediction is largely theoretical[7] and would require the launch[8] of at least three satellites and the creation of a ground-based network that could rapidly process data from space …

Galper said he and his colleagues happened on[9] the possibility of forecasting earthquakes while studying the 600-mile-high radiation belt that encircles the planet's tropical region like a giant doughnut. Early on, they observed an occasional unexpected "bulge"[10] in the belt as particles dipped down—or "fell out"—in the direction of Earth for periods of 10 to 15 minutes. Although sampling of the radiation belt was normally limited to two hours a week, they happened one day in 1985 to record a large amount of "falling out" activity. The same period, they noticed, had been one of high seismic[11] activity on Earth, and they speculated[12] that there could be a connection. In 1989, a seismic measuring station in the San Francisco Bay area near the site of the Loma Prieta [California] earthquake found that electromagnetic waves emanated from the epicenter[13] three hours before the temblor struck. Theorizing that such radiation could affect particle movement in near space, they analyzed the timing of the bulges they had discovered. Galper said that in about 80 out of about 100 cases analyzed, his research team has found a correlation[14] between the unusual behavior of the space particles and the electromagnetic radiation transmitted before major earthquakes.

Because of a time lag[15] of several days in retrieving the data from space, the scientists have never predicted a quake. "Our system is not designed for rapid feeding of information," Galper said …

To establish an earthquake warning system for the entire planet would require a large network of satellites. But Galper said it would be possible to cover the region where 90% of quakes occur—and where most of the world's population lives—with three satellites.

When a satellite detected a bulge in the belt, the information would immediately be routed to a communications satellite that would feed the information to stations on the ground. There, the data would be rapidly processed to estimate the location of the epicenter within an area of 60 square miles. The affected region would be notified and the public would have as much as three hours to prepare for the quake.

[5] ***implausible:*** not likely to be true or possible
[6] ***phenomena:*** facts, events, or images that attract attention
[7] ***theoretical:*** in the world of ideas, not applied in practice
[8] ***launch:*** to send into the air
[9] ***happen on something/happen to do something:*** to find something by chance
[10] ***bulge:*** a rounded projection or swelling
[11] ***seismic:*** related to earthquakes
[12] ***speculate:*** to guess; to theorize using insufficient evidence
[13] ***epicenter:*** the exact center of an earthquake
[14] ***correlation:*** meaningful connection between two events
[15] ***lag:*** delay

1. Several earthquake experts are doubtful about Galper's work. Give at least four reasons for their skepticism.
2. Galper's claims are purely "theoretical" right now. What does this mean?
3. Describe Galper's idea for creating an earthquake warning system.
4. According to the article, are Galper's ideas impossible?

ACTIVITY 10 USING YOUR NOTES

Use your notes to answer the following questions.

1. An earthquake is the v____________________ of the Earth produced by the rapid release of e____________________.
2. Name five different kinds of short-range prediction strategies that researchers have examined.
   a. ____________________
   b. ____________________
   c. ____________________
   d. ____________________
   e. ____________________
3. True or False?
   ____ **a.** Most earthquakes are caused by volcanic eruptions.
   ____ **b.** Chinese seismologists successfully forecast a large earthquake and saved thousands of lives.
   ____ **c.** Since 1975, Chinese seismologists have repeatedly been able to predict serious earthquakes.
   ____ **d.** Researchers who try to make long-range predictions focus on finding historical cycles or patterns.
   ____ **e.** Seismologists found one site in California that has had a serious earthquake every 22 years, without exception.
   ____ **f.** According to the lecturer, almost all seismologists believe that short-term earthquake prediction is difficult, if not impossible.
   ____ **g.** There are more scientists who believe that short-range prediction tools will be found than scientists who believe that long-range prediction tools will be found.
4. In a paragraph on a separate sheet of paper, explain how a flexible stick, a rubber band, and a stone thrown in a pond can demonstrate aspects of the earthquake process.

ACTIVITY 11 COMPARING IDEAS

1. Compare your answers with a partner or group. If you have different answers, check your notes and discuss your reasons for making your choices.
2. Compare your rewritten notes to the sample rewritten notes in Appendix D. Notice the organization. Is yours similar or different? Are your notes equally effective in making important ideas stand out?

ACTIVITY 12 ACADEMIC WORD LIST VOCABULARY

Match the word and its meaning. Write the correct letter in the space provided. Examples are given to help you see words in context.

Group 1

a. possibility (of doing or being something)
b. precise; exact; correct
c. appearing in the future
d. involving strong differences of opinion

___ 1. ***potential*** Earthquakes have the potential to cause extensive damage.

___ 2. ***controversial*** The issue of abortion is quite controversial. There are strong feelings on both sides.

___ 3. ***forthcoming*** Look for that information in my forthcoming article, coming out next month.

___ 4. ***accurate*** We need accurate information about the earthquake's damage.

Group 2

a. a systematic plan to achieve a goal
b. a feature; a part of something (a subject, a topic)
c. an idea that is testable and believed to be true
d. a description of events that create a situation

___ 5. ***theory*** Most of Newton's theories have proven to be correct.

___ 6. ***strategy*** The company asked its salespeople to describe their marketing strategy at their annual meeting.

___ 7. ***scenario*** The president asked us to imagine a scenario that could lead to a more peaceful world.

___ 8. ***aspect*** What aspect of the topic is the speaker going to discuss—the historical, the economic, or the political?

(continued on next page)

Group 3

a. to point out
b. to meet; to come into contact with
c. to watch the progress of
d. to produce

___ 9. *monitor* Doctors monitored the patient's temperature to make sure she was okay.

___ 10. *indicate* The report indicated a serious increase in average temperatures.

___ 11. *encounter* Tell me about the people you encountered during your visit.

___ 12. *generate* The report generated a lot of interest.

ACTIVITY 13 USING VOCABULARY

You will hear vocabulary from the lecture, discussion, and reading in different contexts. Listen and check (✓) the letter of the closest paraphrase of the information.

Group A

1. ___ a. The train goes by at 1:20, 2:20, 3:20, etc.
   ___ b. The train will go by in 20 minutes.
   ___ c. The train goes by every 20 minutes.

2. ___ a. It goes by slowly and never goes close to the speed limit.
   ___ b. It goes by too fast, over the speed limit.
   ___ c. It goes by fast but not over the speed limit.

3. ___ a. Occasionally, the dishes and other objects crack when it passes.
   ___ b. Occasionally, the dishes and other objects shake when it passes.
   ___ c. The dishes and other objects usually aren't affected when it passes.

Group B

1. ___ a. The general wanted the village people to leave before the enemy got there.
   ___ b. The general wanted the village people to stay and fight against the enemy.
   ___ c. The general wanted the village people to make peace with the enemy.

2. ___ a. The problem is that the village is far and has fewer than 1,000 people.

___ b. The problem is that the village is poor and the 1,000 residents are peculiar.

___ c. The problem is that the village is far and has more than 1,000 people.

3. ___ a. The people are frightened because of previous experiences with the general.

___ b. The people are questioning the truth of the general's words because of previous experiences with him.

___ c. The people are angry because of their previous experiences with the general.

4. ___ a. No one can speak to the villagers.

___ b. No one knows what the future will be for the villagers.

___ c. No one knows anyone personally in the village.

ACTIVITY 14 RETAINING VOCABULARY

VOCABULARY LEARNING STRATEGY

Learn synonyms and antonyms in groups.

Write "S" if the word is a synonym. Write "A" if the word is an antonym.

Example

child	S kid	A adult	
1. earthquake	___ seismic activity	___ temblor	___ tremor
2. to shake	___ to tremble	___ to vibrate	___ to steady
3. forthcoming	___ preceding	___ upcoming	___ prior
4. accurate	___ precise	___ exact	___ approximate
5. to monitor	___ to watch	___ to ignore	___ to observe
6. to release	___ to emanate	___ to emit	___ to radiate
7. implausible	___ likely	___ possible	___ unbelievable
8. skeptical	___ questioning	___ doubtful	___ trusting
9. peculiar	___ odd	___ strange	___ weird
10. to foretell	___ to predict	___ to forecast	___ to foresee

ACTIVITY 15 BEYOND THE LECTURE: READING, SPEAKING, AND LISTENING

1. Read an article from the library or the Internet related to earthquakes. Your article might focus on, but doesn't need to be limited to, one of the following:

   - earthquake prediction
   - earthquake historical data
   - country- or region-specific earthquake information
   - earthquake measurement
   - earthquake preparedness
   - earthquake engineering

   Prepare a five-minute presentation. Explain the main ideas of the article and conclude with your opinion and/or evaluation of these ideas.

2. As you listen to your classmates' presentations about their articles, take brief notes. During or after note-taking, write questions to ask your classmate in the left margin of your notes. Then, ask your questions.

TYING IT TOGETHER: END-OF-COURSE EVALUATION

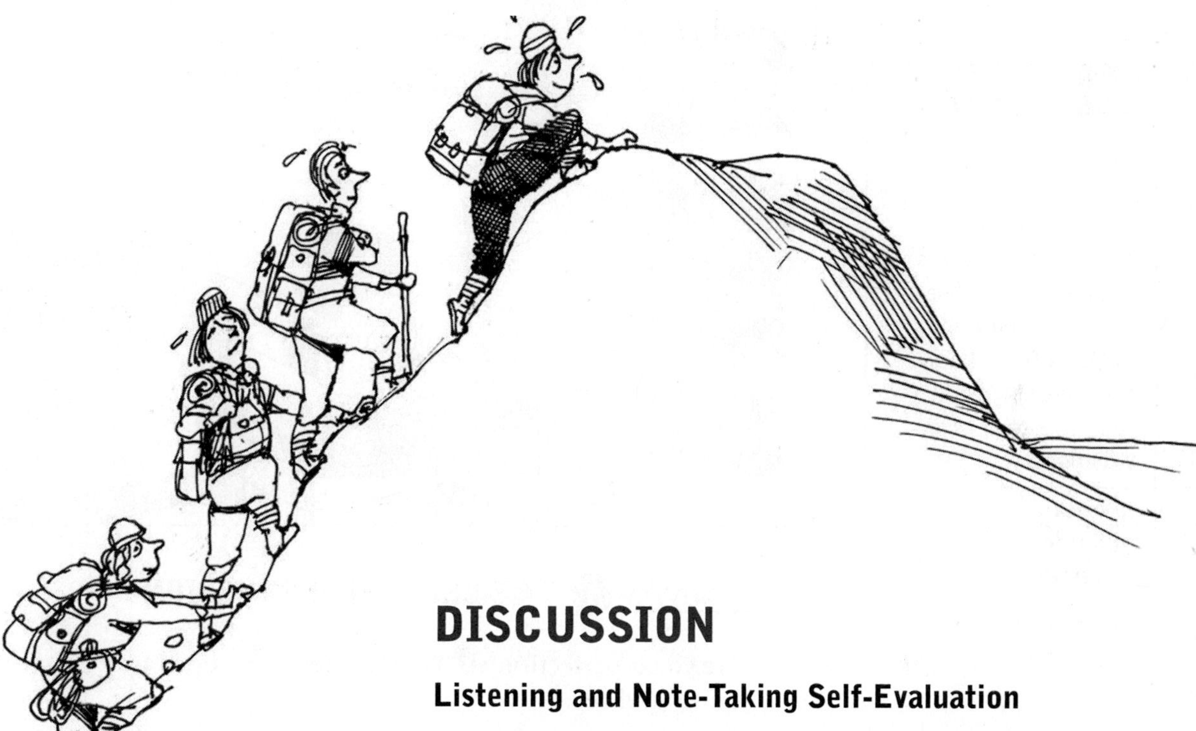

Goals

- Synthesize note-taking skills learned in previous units
- Evaluate listening comprehension, note-taking skills, and inferencing skills through quizzes consisting of true/false, multiple-choice, and short-answer questions
- Evaluate application of listening comprehension and note-taking skills through extended written responses incorporating lecture information

DISCUSSION

Listening and Note-Taking Self-Evaluation

1. Throughout this course, you've studied and practiced specific skills and strategies for listening and note-taking. Talk about the ones that have been most helpful for you.
2. In what ways have your listening and note-taking skills improved?
3. What do you still find challenging about listening and note-taking?
4. What classes might you take in the future in which you will use listening and note-taking skills?
5. Talk about some ways in which your listening and note-taking skills could be important for future jobs you might hold.

In the first unit, you reflected on your listening and note-taking strengths and weaknesses in order to focus your study efforts. Working through this book, you have had a chance to develop your listening and note-taking skills. In this last unit, you will have an opportunity to bring together what you have learned and reevaluate your current skills. For each lecture in this unit, you will take notes, turn them in, and take a quiz on the material a week later, using those notes.

LECTURE 11

Perfectionism (Psychology)

She's trying to draw the perfect circle.

Vocabulary

Related to Achieving

Check (✓) the words you know. Underline the words you want to learn. Then check their meaning with your instructor or in a dictionary.

to excel
to outdo
to surpass

superiority
inferiority

to live up to expectations
to meet expectations
to exceed expectations

to have standards beyond reach

to strive
to push oneself
to be driven

self-worth
self-esteem
self-respect
self-doubt

self-defeating behavior

first-rate
second-rate

ACTIVITY 1 PRE-LECTURE DISCUSSION

Are you a perfectionist? Take this test developed by Dr. David Burns and see.

The Perfectionism Scale

If you are not sure whether you are a perfectionist, you might want to test yourself with Burns's scale. His inventory lists attitudes or beliefs that people sometimes hold. Use the scale below to indicate how much you agree with each statement:

+2	agree strongly
+1	agree
0	neutral
−1	disagree
−2	disagree strongly

Fill in the blank preceding each statement with the number that best describes how you think most of the time. There are no right or wrong answers, so try to respond according to the way you usually feel and behave.

___ **a.** If I don't set the highest standards for myself, I am likely to end up a second-rate person.

___ **b.** People will probably think less of me if I make a mistake.

___ **c.** If I cannot do something really well, there is little point in doing it at all.

___ **d.** I should be upset if I make a mistake.

___ **e.** If I try hard enough, I should be able to excel at anything I attempt.

___ **f.** It is shameful for me to display weaknesses or foolish behavior.

___ **g.** I shouldn't have to repeat the same mistake many times.

___ **h.** An average performance is bound to be unsatisfying to me.

___ **i.** Failing at something important means I'm less of a person.

___ **j.** If I scold myself for failing to live up to my expectations, it will help me to do better in the future.

SCORING: *Add up your scores for all items, noting that plus numbers and minus numbers cancel each other out. For example, if your answer on five items was +1 and your score on the other five was –1, your total test score would be 0. If you answered +2 on all the items, your total score would be +20, revealing a very high degree of perfectionism. If you answered –2 on every item, your score would be –20, signifying a strongly nonperfectionistic mindset. Preliminary studies suggest that about half of the [American] population is likely to score from +2 to +16, indicating varying degrees of perfectionism.*

Share your results with your classmates.

Divide the class into two groups: those who scored on the higher end of the perfectionist scale and those who scored on the lower end. In the groups, discuss the following questions.

1. Do you think you are in the right group? Why or why not?
2. Using your own words, define *perfectionism*.
3. Do you think that your degree of perfectionism helps or hinders your success? Why?

Compare each group's ideas.

ACTIVITY 2 PREPARING FOR THE LECTURE

This lecture is about the costs and benefits of perfectionistic attitudes. Before listening to the lecture, write your ideas about each question in the column marked "My Ideas." Discuss your answers with your classmates. (Ignore the column marked "The Lecturer's Ideas" for now.)

	MY IDEAS	THE LECTURER'S IDEAS
1. Is a perfectionist attitude a positive or negative trait?		
2. What is "perfectionism"?		
3. Do you think it would help you or hurt you to have a perfectionist attitude in the business world? Why?		
4. Do you think it would help you or hurt you to have a perfectionist attitude in the athletic world? Why?		
5. Do you think it would help you or hurt you to have a perfectionist attitude in the world of education? Why?		
6. Are there emotional costs of perfectionist attitudes? If so, what are they?		
7. Are there physical costs of perfectionist attitudes? If so, what are they?		
8. Where do perfectionist attitudes come from?		

ACTIVITY 3 LISTENING FOR THE LARGER PICTURE

Listen to the lecture once without taking notes. Discuss with your classmates how the lecturer answered the questions in Activity 2.

How did your ideas compare with the lecturer's ideas?

ACTIVITY 4 DEFINING VOCABULARY

The following words and expressions were used in the lecture. You may remember the contexts in which you heard them. Listen to another example of each word or expression in a new context. Check (✓) the letter of the definition that most closely matches what you think the word or expression means.

1. *compulsive*
   ___ **a.** feeling pulled to do something and unable to stop
   ___ **b.** feeling angry and ready to fight with others
   ___ **c.** feeling outgoing and energetic in all social situations

2. *"pursuit* of excellence"*
   ___ **a.** the failure to win in a competition among the best
   ___ **b.** the desire to find high-quality goods to purchase
   ___ **c.** the attempt to reach the highest limits of our possibilities

3. *strain*
   ___ **a.** to hurt oneself physically because of an accident
   ___ **b.** to push oneself with great effort
   ___ **c.** to pretend to listen to someone

4. *be plagued by self-doubt*
   ___ **a.** to be repeatedly bothered by a lack of self-confidence
   ___ **b.** to sometimes be bothered by a lack of self-confidence
   ___ **c.** to have a great deal of self-confidence, increasing over time

5. *anticipate* (something)*
   ___ **a.** to ignore; to not pay attention to something
   ___ **b.** to expect something to happen
   ___ **c.** to be involved in; to participate in something

6. *defensive*
   ___ **a.** acting in an aggressive and violent manner
   ___ **b.** behaving in a way that suggests depression or unhappiness
   ___ **c.** taking an attitude of protecting oneself against attack or danger

(continued on next page)

7. *frustrate*

___ a. to test someone's ability so that he can measure his intelligence and skill

___ b. to make someone feel so involved that he loses a sense of time passing

___ c. to make someone feel upset because of an inability to achieve a goal

8. *alienate (others)*

___ a. to make others feel distant

___ b. to impress others so that they feel great respect

___ c. to bring people together; to unite people

9. *"cream of the crop"*

___ a. the best of a group

___ b. athletes of different skill levels

___ c. the average in a group

10. *dichotomy*

___ a. a form of government in which one person rules with unreasonable power

___ b. a classification focusing on the similarities between two things

___ c. a division into two parts, especially opposites

11. *reach "the point of diminishing* returns"*

___ a. to reach a point at which extra work doesn't bring enough benefits in light of the required effort

___ b. to reach a point at which one should "start from scratch," on a project (i.e., start all over again from the beginning)

___ c. to reach a point of limited self-confidence and fear of failure

12. *distort**

___ a. to reflect clearly and accurately

___ b. to have a poor sense of oneself; to have no self-confidence

___ c. to misrepresent or change the shape of something

13. *be preoccupied with deadlines*

___ a. to take care of responsibilities before their due dates

___ b. to have one's mind fixed on certain due dates

___ c. to be irresponsible and forgetful about certain due dates

14. *traits*

___ a. exchanges; swaps

___ b. words that make someone feel scared

___ c. qualities; characteristics

ACTIVITY 5 LISTENING AND NOTE-TAKING

Listen to the lecture a second time and take notes. Then review and revise your notes. Add information that you remember. Consider rewriting your notes. Make the relationship between ideas clear and make important ideas stand out. Hand your notes in to your teacher.

In about a week, your teacher will return your notes and give you a quiz on the information in the lecture. The purpose of this activity is to find out how well your notes help you to retain information.

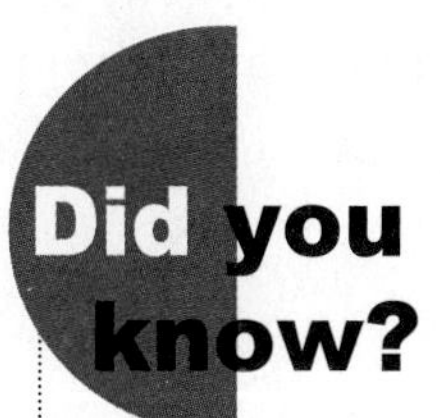

Thomas Edison made 1,000 unsuccessful attempts at inventing the light bulb. When a reporter asked, "How did it feel to fail 1,000 times?" Edison replied, "I didn't fail 1,000 times. The light bulb was an invention with 1,000 steps."

ACTIVITY 6 POST-LECTURE READING AND DISCUSSION

Discuss the following in small groups.

1. Psychologists point out that there is a difference between "healthy striving" and "perfectionism." The following excerpt is from a publication by the University of Illinois at Urbana-Champaign's Counseling Center.

Healthy goal setting and striving[1] are quite different from the self-defeating[2] process of perfectionism. Healthy strivers tend to set goals based on their own wants and desires rather than primarily in response to external expectations. Their goals are usually just one step beyond what they have already accomplished. In other words, their goals are realistic, internal, and potentially attainable.[3] Healthy strivers take pleasure in the process of pursuing[4] the task at hand rather than focusing only on the end result. When they experience disapproval or failure, their reactions are generally limited to specific situations rather than generalized to their entire self-worth.

[1] *to strive:* to work hard for something
[2] *self-defeating:* acting against one's own interests
[3] *to attain:* to reach; to achieve
[4] *to pursue:* to take steps to reach or complete (a goal, a task)

Each sentence in the previous paragraph (except the first one) either implies or explicitly states a contrast between healthy goal setting and perfectionism. Write these differences in the chart.

HEALTHY STRIVERS	PERFECTIONISTS
• set goals based on own wants and desires	• set goals in response to external expectations

2. Do you think you are more of a healthy striver or a perfectionist? Use examples from your life to explain your answer.

3. The lecturer ends with suggestions for dealing with perfectionism. Read the longer list of suggestions that follows from the same publication. Then discuss your reactions to each suggestion. Do you think it is useful? Why or why not? Which suggestion would you most like to incorporate into your own life?

What to Do about Perfectionism

The first step in changing from perfectionistic attitudes to healthy striving is to realize that perfectionism is undesirable. Perfection is an illusion[1] that is unattainable. The next step is to challenge the self-defeating thoughts and behaviors that fuel[2] perfectionism. Some of the following strategies may help:

- Set realistic and reachable goals based on your own wants and needs and what you have accomplished in the past. This will enable you to achieve and also will lead to a greater sense of self-esteem.[3]
- Set subsequent[4] goals in a sequential manner. As you reach a goal, set your next goal one level beyond your present level of accomplishment.
- Experiment with your standards for success. Choose any activity and instead of aiming for 100%, try for 90%, 80%, or even 60% success. This will help you to realize that the world does not end when you are not perfect.
- Focus on the process of doing an activity, not just on the end result. Evaluate your success not only in terms of what you accomplished but also in terms of how much you enjoyed the task. Recognize that there can be value in the process of pursuing a goal.
- Use feelings of anxiety and depression as opportunities to ask yourself, "Have I set up impossible expectations for myself in this situation?"
- Confront[5] the fears that may be behind your perfectionism by asking yourself, "What am I afraid of? What is the worst thing that could happen?"
- Recognize that many positive things can be learned only by making mistakes. When you make a mistake, ask, "What can I learn from this experience?" More specifically, think of a recent mistake you have made and list all the things you can learn from it.
- Avoid "all-or-nothing" thinking in relation to your goals. Learn to discriminate[6] the tasks you want to give high priority from those tasks that are less important to you. On less important tasks, choose to put forth less effort.

[1] ***illusion:*** a fantasy; a false view of reality
[2] ***fuel:*** to energize
[3] ***self-esteem:*** self-confidence
[4] ***subsequent:*** following
[5] ***confront:*** to face; to deal with directly
[6] ***discriminate:*** to see the difference between

ACTIVITY 7 PREPARING FOR THE QUIZ

STUDY STRATEGY

Prepare yourself for tests by predicting questions (short-answer, true/false, multiple-choice, fill-in-the-blank, essay) that you expect the professor to ask. Review with classmates, taking turns asking and answering these questions.

Write five questions that you think the professor might ask on the quiz. Do you and your classmates have similar or different questions? Which ones seem likeliest to be on a quiz?

ACTIVITY 8 BEYOND THE LECTURE: WRITING

Write about one of the following topics.

1. Write an essay about an educational system that you know well. In what ways does this system encourage or discourage perfectionism? In what ways does it encourage or discourage healthy striving? Use information from the lecture and readings to support your ideas.

2. Write an essay about a culture that you know well. In what ways does this culture encourage or discourage perfectionism? In what ways does it encourage or discourage healthy striving? Use information from the lecture and readings to support your ideas.

3. Imagine that you are a school administrator. You want to educate parents about the dangers of pushing their children to become perfectionists. Write a letter to parents to persuade them that perfectionism will not help their children succeed. Use specific evidence from the lecture to support your ideas.

4. Write a response paper that presents your perspective on the information presented in this lecture unit. Synthesize, evaluate, and give your opinion on the information presented.

LECTURE 12

High Tech Harvesting: Hope or Horror? (Agriculture, Ecology, Biology)

Vocabulary

Related to Agriculture

Check (✓) the words you know. Underline the words you want to learn. Then check their meaning with your instructor or in a dictionary.

to plow
to fertilize
to irrigate
to harvest
to rotate crops

pests, pesticide
insects, insecticide
weeds, herbicide

organic farming

subsistence farming

fertilizers
fertile land
barren/depleted land

soil, earth, dirt

seeds
pollen, to pollinate
to breed
to cross-breed

hybrid plants
inbred plants

ACTIVITY 1 PRE-LECTURE DISCUSSION

1. Imagine what the customer is thinking. What would you think if you were in that restaurant?

2. Talk about your food shopping and eating habits. For example: What percentage of the time do you buy organic food? How often do you eat junk food? Do you read food labels when you shop? Do you worry about pesticides on your fresh fruit and vegetables? Do you drink bottled water? Are you a vegetarian?

3. Do you trust the quality of the food that you eat? Why or why not?

ACTIVITY 2 PREPARING FOR THE LECTURE

In this talk, there is a lot of information about "genetic engineering," or "the alteration of genetic material by direct intervention in genetic processes with the purpose of producing new substances or improving functions of existing organisms."[1] Listen to an excerpt from the lecture in which the professor reviews some basics of genetics. Then answer the questions below.

1. Match the words with a definition.

___ **chromosome**	**a.** a molecule that carries genetic information
___ **gene**	**b.** a unit that determines a living thing's hereditary characteristics. It is made up of DNA.
___ **DNA**	**c.** a structure that consists of DNA, proteins, and thousands of genes. Humans have 46 of them, 23 from each parent.

2. What does the lecturer think is amazing about DNA?

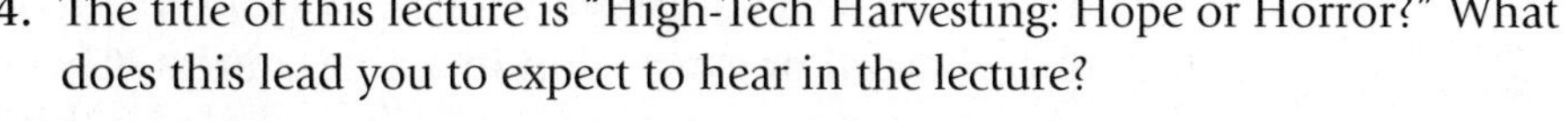

3. If DNA contains the same ingredients across life forms, what accounts for the differences among life forms, according to the lecturer? Check (✓) as many as are appropriate.

   ___ **a.** the amount of the DNA

   ___ **b.** the arrangement of components of the DNA

   ___ **c.** the shape of the DNA

   ___ **d.** the number of chromosomes

4. The title of this lecture is "High-Tech Harvesting: Hope or Horror?" What does this lead you to expect to hear in the lecture?

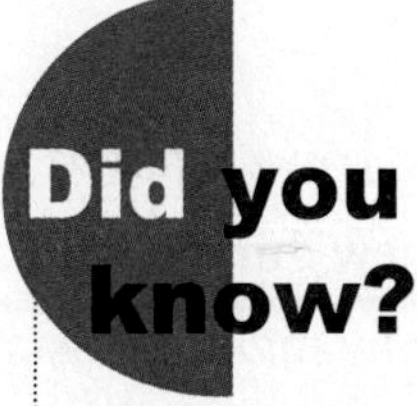

One person's DNA is 99.9% the same as another's (except for identical twins, whose genes are 100% the same). What a difference 0.1% can make!

[1] http://www.answers.com/topic/geneticengineering

ACTIVITY 3 LISTENING FOR THE LARGER PICTURE

Listen to the lecture once without taking notes. Check (✓) the information that the professor gave in the lecture.

___ a. the history of farming

___ b. the most important scientists working in the field of genetic engineering

___ c. the benefits of using chemical fertilizers and pesticides

___ d. the drawbacks of using chemical fertilizers and pesticides

___ e. decade when the use of chemical fertilizers and pesticides was introduced

___ f. statistics on worldwide use of chemical pesticides

___ g. reasons why crop rotation is useful

___ h. an example of specific crops that are often rotated

___ i. three types of genetic engineering of plants

___ j. a definition of transgenic plants

___ k. the specific steps for transferring DNA from one species to another

___ l. pros and cons of genetic engineering

___ m. the lecturer's opinion of genetic engineering

ACTIVITY 4 DEFINING VOCABULARY

The following words and expressions were used in the lecture. You may remember the contexts in which you heard them. Listen to another example of each word or expression in a new context. Check (✓) the letter of the definition that most closely matches what you think the word or expression means.

1. *trial and error*

   ___ a. a process of going to court to prove one's innocence

   ___ b. a process of trying new things and learning from mistakes

   ___ c. a process of repeatedly making mistakes and never learning from them

2. *drawback*

   ___ a. unusual characteristic

   ___ b. artistic talent; creativity

   ___ c. limitation; disadvantage

3. *disrupt*

____ a. to travel long distances by airplane

____ b. to break the flow or usual pattern

____ c. to explode (with strong emotions)

4. *proliferate*

____ a. to kill in large quantities

____ b. to pay attention for long periods of time

____ c. to multiply; to increase in large numbers

5. *resistance*

____ a. the ability to remain unhurt by disease or attack

____ b. the development of healthy eating habits

____ c. the desire to do something repeatedly

6. *toxic*

____ a. highly effective

____ b. poisonous

____ c. expensive

7. *modification*

____ a. change; alteration

____ b. enjoyment; relaxation

____ c. destruction; elimination

8. *an advocate*

____ a. a farm worker

____ b. an opponent

____ c. a supporter

9. *malnutrition*

____ a. a state of health caused by good eating habits

____ b. a condition caused by lack of healthy food

____ c. an illness characterized by overeating

10. *deficiency*

____ a. surplus; excessive amounts

____ b. effectiveness; producing the desired amount

____ c. lack; insufficient amount

(continued on next page)

11. *vaccines*

____ a. paperwork showing classes that have been completed

____ b. school uniforms, designed for strength and comfort

____ c. medication that makes one safe from a specific disease

12. *allergy*

____ a. attraction to a substance or animal

____ b. fear of a substance or animal

____ c. high sensitivity to a substance or animal

13. *sue*

____ a. to do nothing in response to a wrongdoing

____ b. to express one's gratitude and appreciation

____ c. to file a lawsuit (to protect one's rights)

14. *"err on the side of caution"*

____ a. to do what is safe instead of taking a risk

____ b. to make mistakes because of not being careful

____ c. to take chances instead of always doing what is safe

ACTIVITY 5 LISTENING AND NOTE-TAKING

Listen to the lecture a second time and take notes. Then review and revise your notes. Add information that you remember. If helpful, consider rewriting your notes. Make the relationship between ideas clear and make important ideas stand out. Hand your notes in to your teacher.

In about a week, your teacher will return your notes and give you a quiz on the information in the lecture.

ACTIVITY 6 POST-LECTURE READING AND DISCUSSION

The Union of Concerned Scientists is a science-based nonprofit organization working for a healthy environment and a safer world. Read how they describe "genetic engineering" on their Web site.[1]

[1] http://www.ucsusa.org/food_and_environment/genetic_engineering/what-is-genetic-engineering.html (Union of Concerned Scientists)

Genetic engineering refers to a set of technologies that are being used to change the genetic makeup of cells and move genes across species boundaries[1] to produce novel[2] organisms. The techniques involve highly sophisticated[3] manipulations[4] of genetic material and other biologically important chemicals.

Genes are the chemical blueprints[5] that determine an organism's traits.[6] Moving genes from one organism to another transfers those traits. Through genetic engineering, organisms are given new combinations of genes—and therefore new combinations of traits—that do not occur in nature and, indeed, cannot be developed by natural means. Such an artificial technology is radically different from traditional plant and animal breeding.

Nature can produce organisms with new gene combinations through sexual reproduction. A brown cow bred to a yellow cow may produce a calf of a completely new color. But reproductive mechanisms limit the number of new combinations. Cows must breed with other cows (or very near relatives). A breeder who wants a purple cow would be able to breed toward one only if the necessary purple genes were available somewhere in a cow or a near relative to cows. A genetic engineer has no such restriction. If purple genes are available anywhere in nature—in a sea urchin or an iris—those genes could be used in attempts to produce purple cows. This unprecedented[7] ability to shuffle[8] genes means that genetic engineers can concoct[9] gene combinations that would never be found in nature.

[1] ***boundary:*** limits
[2] ***novel:*** new and unusual
[3] ***sophisticated:*** complex and advanced
[4] ***manipulation:*** handling and repositioning
[5] ***blueprint:*** a detailed drawing or design showing how to do something
[6] ***trait:*** characteristic
[7] ***unprecedented:*** never having happened before
[8] ***shuffle:*** to mix in a different order
[9] ***concoct:*** to invent (something strange)

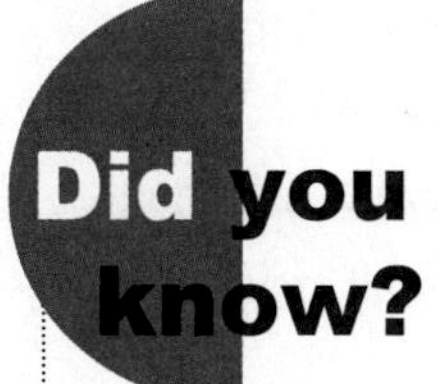

Did you know only 3% of the earth's surface can grow food?

Work in small groups to discuss the following.

1. For the moment, don't think about whether genetic engineering is desirable. Use your imagination. Dream up five fun or useful genetically engineered products (e.g., broccoli that looks and tastes like chocolate; a cat with the personality of a dog; a person with the eyesight of an eagle). Talk about what would be special about those products. When you finish, do the opposite: think of five "nightmare" genetically engineered products (e.g., a mosquito with an elephant's growth gene; perfume that smells like fish). Talk about why these would be so horrifying.
2. Having listened to the lecture and heard about the arguments for and against genetic engineering, where do you stand on the issue? Why?

STUDY STRATEGY

Start reviewing your notes days before a test (or longer, depending on the size of the test). Review regularly and especially, shortly before the test.

ACTIVITY 7 PREPARING FOR THE QUIZ

Write five questions that you think the professor might ask on the quiz. Do you and your classmates have similar or different questions? Which ones seem likeliest to be on the quiz?

ACTIVITY 8 BEYOND THE LECTURE: POLLING

Different polling organizations have surveyed Americans to find out their views of genetically engineered crops and food. Listed below are some questions that have been asked.[1] Answer the questions yourself first. Then find out your classmates' answers and calculate statistics for your class.

1. As you may know, some food products and medicines are being developed using new scientific techniques. The general area is called "biotechnology" and includes tools such as genetic engineering and genetic modification of food. How closely have you been following the news about this issue: very closely, somewhat closely, not too closely, or not at all?[1]

   ____ very closely ____ somewhat closely

   ____ not too closely ____ not at all

2. How likely do you think it is that the following will happen because of the use of new types of plants and crops developed by genetic engineering?[2]

   a. "Food based on these new crops will be poisonous or cause diseases in people who eat them."

   ____ very likely ____ somewhat likely

   ____ not very likely ____ not at all likely

   ____ unsure

   b. "They will upset the balance of nature and damage the environment."

   ____ very likely ____ somewhat likely

   ____ not very likely ____ not at all likely

   ____ unsure

   c. "They will make food less expensive than it would be otherwise."

   ____ very likely ____ somewhat likely

   ____ not very likely ____ not at all likely

   ____ unsure

3. As far as you know, have you ever eaten genetically modified foods?[3]

   ____ yes ____ no ____ don't know

4. When you go to the grocery store, how important is it to you to know whether a product contains genetically modified agricultural products?[4]

   ____ very important ____ somewhat important

   ____ not too important ____ not at all important

   ____ don't know

[1] *Gallup 2005*
[2] *Harris 2000*
[3] *Pew Initiative on Food and Technology Poll 2001*
[4] *Pew Initiative on Food and Technology Poll 2001*

[1] *All polls cited here can be found at http://www.pollingreport.com/science.htm.*

5. To the best of your knowledge, how much of the food in a typical American grocery store is genetically modified—that is, food modified through biotechnology—or contains genetically modified ingredients? [5]

____ less than 25%

____ 25% to 50%

____ 50% to 75%

____ more than 75%

____ don't know

6. How safe do you think genetically modified foods are?[6]

____ basically safe

____ basically unsafe

____ don't know

7. Do you think foods that contain genetically modified ingredients should be labeled indicating that, or don't you think that is necessary?[7]

____ should be labeled

____ not necessary

____ unsure

8. How likely is it that you would buy food that is labeled as having been genetically modified? [8]

____ very likely

____ somewhat likely

____ not very likely

____ not at all likely

____ unsure

9. Overall, do you support or oppose the use of biotechnology in agriculture and food production?[9]

____ strongly support

____ moderately support

____ moderately oppose

____ strongly oppose

____ unsure

10. Overall, do you think the benefits of developing and growing these new plants and crops outweigh the risks of doing this, or do you think the risks outweigh the benefits?[10]

____ benefits outweigh the risks

____ risks outweigh the benefits

____ not sure

[5] *Pew Initiative on Food and Technology Poll 2001*
[6] *Pew Initiative on Food and Technology Poll 2001*
[7] *CBS 2008*
[8] *CBS 2008*
[9] *Gallup 2005*
[10] *Harris 2000*

Now find out what others outside of your class think. Do the activities below and discuss your findings and responses.

1. Individually, interview five people outside of your class using the same set of questions. Note their nationalities and responses. Pool your results with others in your class and calculate statistics.
2. Review the results of these polls when Americans were surveyed by professional polling organizations. How did your poll results compare to these?
3. Was anything in these polls surprising or disturbing or odd? Were the results of these polls as you expected? Write a reaction to the findings of these different polls.

APPENDIX A Academic Word List Vocabulary

The following words come from the Academic Word List (AWL). The numbers in parentheses indicate the lectures where the words are used.

abstract (8)
accurate (10)
achieve/
achievement (6)
acknowledge/
acknowledgement (5)
adjustment (4)
alter/alteration (7)
analytical (8)
anticipate (11)
apparent (8)
appreciation (8)
approach (8)
appropriate (7)
aspect (10)
assist/assistance (7)
assumption (9)
automatic (9)
aware (9)

behalf (5)
benefit (6) (7)

commodity (9)
community (4)
component (8)
concept (9)
consult/consultation (5)
context (9)
contrary (8)
contract (9)
controversy (10)
cyclical (10)

debate (6)
demonstrate/
demonstration (9)
device (3) (7)
devote/devotion (6)
dimension (7)
diminish (11)
distribute/
distribution (6)
distort (11)
diverse (4)

element (8)
encounter (10)
entity (9)
equipped (7)
erode (6)
ethnic (4)
eventual (4)
exceed (10)
expand/expansion (5)
explicit (8)
expose (7)
external (9)
extract (3)

factor (4)
focus (4)
forthcoming (10)
found (5)

generation (7)/
generate (10)
global (6)
grant (9)

identity (4)
image (7)
impact (6)
imply (8)
impose (9)
indicate (10)
individuality (4)
insight (8)
interaction (8)
internalize (9)
investigate/
investigation (5)
involve/involvement (6)
isolate/isolation (5)

justify/justification (5)

labor (7)
layer (8)

major (3)/majority (4)
manual (3)
monitor (10)

network (5)

obvious (3) (7)
overall (8)
overlap (8)

parallel (8)
participate/
participation (5)
persist/persistence (6)
perspective (8)
phenomenon (3)
philosophy (8)
potential (10)
precede (6)
precise/precision (7)
proceed (3)
promote/promotion (6)
pursue/pursuit (5) (11)

quotation/quote (6)

(ir)rational (7)
regional (4)
reinforce (9)
release (10)
relevant (3)
rely (3)
require/requirement (5)
restore (6)
restrain (9)
retain/retention (7)
revolutionize (3)
rigid (9)

scenario (10)
scope (8)
security (9)
sequence (3)
significant (9)
sole (5)
source (10)
strategy (10)
survival/survive (5)

task (7)
theory (10)
transmit/
transmission (7)
trend (4)

undergo (7)

variable/vary (7)
vehicle (3)
violate/violation (5) (9)

whereas (9)

APPENDIX B Lecture Index by Organizational Plan

The organizational plan indicated occurs in either the entire lecture or a significant part of it.

Organizational Plan	Lecture Number and Title	
Defining a Term	LECTURE 7:	Paging Robodoc: Robots in Medicine
	LECTURE 9:	Hall's Classification of Cultures
	LECTURE 11:	Perfectionism
	LECTURE 12:	High-Tech Harvesting: Hope or Horror?
Listing Subtopics	LECTURE 1:	Academic Listening
	LECTURE 2:	Women and Work
	LECTURE 5:	Amnesty International
	LECTURE 6:	Two 21st Century Eco-Heroes
	LECTURE 11:	Perfectionism
	LECTURE 12:	High-Tech Harvesting: Hope or Horror?
Describing a Causal Relationship	LECTURE 10:	Earthquakes: Can They Be Predicted?
	LECTURE 11:	Perfectionism
	LECTURE 12:	High-Tech Harvesting: Hope or Horror?
Exemplifying a Topic	LECTURE 5:	Amnesty International
	LECTURE 6:	Two 21st Century Eco-Heroes
	LECTURE 7:	Paging Robodoc: Robots in Medicine
	LECTURE 8:	How to Look at Art
	LECTURE 9:	Hall's Classification of Cultures
Describing a Process or Sequence of Events	LECTURE 3:	Milestones in Technology
	LECTURE 4:	Immigration to the United States
	LECTURE 7:	Paging Robodoc: Robots in Medicine
	LECTURE 10:	Earthquakes: Can They Be Predicted?
	LECTURE 11:	Perfectionism
	LECTURE 12:	High-Tech Harvesting: Hope or Horror?
Classifying Subtopics	LECTURE 4:	Immigration to the United States
	LECTURE 8:	How to Look at Art
	LECTURE 9:	Hall's Classification of Cultures
	LECTURE 10:	Earthquakes: Can They Be Predicted?
	LECTURE 11:	Perfectionism
	LECTURE 12:	High-Tech Harvesting: Hope or Horror?
Describing Characteristics	LECTURE 7:	Paging Robodoc: Robots in Medicine
	LECTURE 8:	How to Look at Art
Comparing and Contrasting	LECTURE 1:	The Process of Lecture Comprehension
	LECTURE 2:	Women and Work
	LECTURE 9:	Hall's Classification of Cultures
	LECTURE 11:	Perfectionism
Making a Generalization and Providing Evidence	LECTURE 10:	Earthquakes: Can They Be Predicted?
	LECTURE 11:	Perfectionism

SUBJECT MATTER	LECTURE NUMBER AND TITLE	
Social Sciences and Humanities		
Art	LECTURE 8:	How to Look at Art
History	LECTURE 4:	Immigration to the United States
Linguistics	LECTURE 1:	Academic Listening
Political Science	LECTURE 5:	Amnesty International
	LECTURE 6:	Two 21st Century Eco-Heroes
Psychology	LECTURE 2:	Women and Work
	LECTURE 9:	Hall's Classification of Cultures
	LECTURE 11:	Perfectionism
Sociology	LECTURE 2:	Women and Work
	LECTURE 4:	Immigration to the United States
	LECTURE 9:	Hall's Classification of Cultures
Sciences		
Agriculture	LECTURE 12:	High-Tech Harvesting: Hope or Horror?
Biology	LECTURE 7:	Paging Robodoc: Robots in Medicine
	LECTURE 12:	High-Tech Harvest: Hope or Horror?
Computer Science/Technology	LECTURE 3:	Milestones in Technology
	LECTURE 7:	Paging Robodoc: Robots in Medicine
Ecology	LECTURE 6:	Two 21st Century Eco-Heroes
	LECTURE 12:	High-Tech Harvest: Hope or Horror?
Food Sciences	LECTURE 12:	High-Tech Harvest: Hope or Horror?
Geology	LECTURE 10:	Earthquakes: Can They Be Predicted?
Business/Management		
Organizational Systems	LECTURE 5:	Amnesty International
	LECTURE 11:	Perfectionism

LECTURE 5 Amnesty International

Amnesty International (AI)

— founded in 1961

— one of largest human rights org.

2008 — 2,200,000 members in 150 countries

— 1977 — Nobel Peace Prize

— 1978 — award by UN

Concerned only w/prisoners

— wants to release prisoners of conscience — "person detained for non-violent expression of polit. or religious beliefs or for color, ethnicity, race, sex"

— wants fair trials for all

— against torture

— against death penalty

8 Principles of AI:

1. limited mandate

   — does not work for all human rights — just concentrates on polit. prisoners, torture, execution

2. focus on indiv. prisoner

   — wants specific details about indiv. not just general info.

   — AI adoption groups — groups of indiv. who work for indiv. prisoners

3. action grounded in fact

   — wants reliable info. ∴ research

4. based on member participation

   — AI believes indiv. makes difference

   — no human rights protection if left to govt. alone

   — AI built on indiv. effort

(continued on next page)

5. moral suasion w/govt.
   - doesn't want conflict — seeks dialogue
   - doesn't want sanctions against govt.
   - wants feedback on reports from govt.
6. impartial in work
   - doesn't matter about politics, religion, ideology; AI works everywhere
   - won't compare/rank countries
7. independent in policy & finance
   - no links to state, polit. body, ideology, religion
   - only authority is membership
   - rules to protect independence
     - if have high post in govt., cannot have high post in AI
     - can't work for prisoners in own country
   - all finances from subscriptions
     - no gifts w/"strings"
     - no grants from govt. except relief
8. committed to intl. responsibility for human rights
   - human rights everyone's responsibility
   - not just own country's concern

Example of Work:

- letter writing campaigns began 1961
- Urgent Action Network – emergency letters
  - first one, Brazil w/ military regime, 1972
  - Luiz Rossi arrested w/o explan. 2/73
  - wife expected killed but alive, freed 10/73
    - Y? AI letters from world

LECTURE 6 Two 21st Century Eco-Heroes

Nobel Prizes (given since 1901)

Types: Chemistry, Literature, Physics, Peace, Medicine

Alfred Nobel: born Sweden 1800s, inventor, scientist

Left fortune to prize for people who benefit mankind

<u>2 recent winners of Peace Prize (for work in ecology!)</u>

Note shift in thinking: in past, peace = prevent war

Now, incl. ecological work

Was this Nobel's intention? Maybe not.

<u>Wangari Maathai</u>: 2004: first ♀ fr. Africa to get Nobel Peace Prize

Born Kenya 1940

Biologist. first ♀ in E. & Cent. Af. to receive PhD; first ♀ prof. at U of Nairobi

Fights for democratic rights, esp. for ♀; social, ec. & cult. development in Africa

Esp. environment:

Saw problem of deforestation & soil erosion

1950-2000, Kenya lost 90% of forests.

1977: resigned prof. job & founded grassroots movement to plant trees

Green Belt Movement

Largely poor ♀ planting trees 1 by 1

Why? Prevent desertification (lose farmable land to deserts)

Restore forests

End peverty

Improve ♀ lives

Tree ♀

(continued on next page)

Other work:

1980s, one leader of pro-democracy movement. → imprisoned & attacked for beliefs.

2002, elected to Parliament

2003, Minister of Environment....

founded Kenyan Green Party

<u>Al Gore Jr.</u>, 2007 prize

American, born 1948

lawyer

VP of US (Clinton yrs.).

Since 2000: esp. known for campaign on global warming

gradual heating of the Earth leading to climate change and rising sea levels caused by burning fossil fuels (e.g. coal, oil, natural gas).

→ serious consequences: affects agriculture, wildlife, weather.

says "planetary emergency"

won Nobel for persistent work educating abt. this

Made movie 2007 "An Inconvenient Truth" abt. prob. (won Acad. Award)

Nobel Prize: Making connection: peace and environmental work!

LECTURE 7 Paging Robodoc: Robots in Medicine

Robot: word fr. Czech "forced labor"

Robot Industries Assoc. definition: "a reprogrammable, multifunctional, manipulator designed to move material, parts, tools, or specialized devices through variable programmed motions to perform a variety of tasks"

"reprogrammable" — can get new instructions

"multifunctional" — can perform variety of tasks

How robots work:

— microprocessor is "brain"

— most robots have single hand & arm (w/5 or 6 joints):

"end effector" (sometimes w/2 "fingers," sometimes just tools)

Robots use in hospitals: e.g., Robodoc

— first generation robot tech. in hospitals

— more precise & steady than humans

— esp. useful in hip replacement

Why? Surgery is physically laborious

high # of this surgery

in past — surgeons manually carved cavity & bore holes in thighbone

— resulted in rough fit for implant

— used cement to hold implant but cement lost grip (after 5–10 yrs) & many needed surgery again

w/Robodoc — computer image finds exact size of cavity for implant

— Robodoc makes hole; implant fits exactly

Process of hip replacement surgery w/Robodoc (~ 90 min.)

— surgeon takes CT scan of femur

— " " transfers image to computer

— " " views image & chooses implant (from computer memory)

— " " stores info. in computer

— in operating room, surgeon exposes femur

— computer gives robot instructions about cavity & implant

— Robodoc drills cavity

— after ~ 20 min., surgeon fits implant & completes surgery

Some resistance to robots:

— fear robots will replace surgeons

— fear robots will "go crazy"

developers emphasize robots ASSIST surgeons, not replace

+ lots of safety controls

LECTURE 8 How to Look at Art

Directed Looking

— way to <u>look</u> at art

— involves examining works directly (not reading about work or studying history)

Components of "directed looking" approach: 5 categories of observation (in real life, categories overlap)

1. Observing physical properties
   e.g., size? mediums? how mediums applied? textures? 2-D or 3-D?

2. Exploring subject matter — need to examine representative and abstract
   - representative (still life, portrait, etc.)
   - sometimes subject matter more than just objects
     - e.g., Van Gogh's <u>Hospital Corridor</u>
       - represents hall
       - subject matter not hall... maybe fear? confusion?
   - abstract
     e.g., Kline — <u>Painting #2</u> — maybe about growth? progress?

3. Observing illusionary properties — how artist makes us believe something impossible (e.g., 3-D on 2-D paper, distance)
   - create 3-D through shading, highlighting
     (Callahan photo, no shading ∴ seems "flat")
   - techniques for creating illusion of distance?
     - smaller seems farther (e.g., door in Van Gogh's <u>Hospital</u>)
     - out of focus seems farther

4. Observing formal elements (line, color, shape, composition)

how line (explicit & implied), color, shape arranged

how space & shapes interact

focal points

— e.g., lines — heavy? light? choppy?

— explicit lines? e.g., Hopper (Early Sunday Morning)

— implied lines? e.g., Lange (Migrant Mother) — implied diagonal up arm to face

— shapes? touching? overlapping?

— e.g., Hopper (full of rectangles, squares — represent regularity of life?)

— colors? realistic? effects?

— e.g., Hopper painting — bright yellow shades stand out against dark

5. Observing viewer perspective — where artist positions viewer

— e.g., looking at object from below? above? equal level? from far? near?

— Degas' Orchestra of Opera — viewer looks up at stage

LECTURE 9 Hall's Classification of Culture

Edward Hall — anthropologist — works w/Am. Indian

- studies relation betw. cultures, not just culture
- believes diff. cultures have diff. assumptions about time, space, relations
- classifies culture on continuum — high/low context

HALL'S CLASSIFICATION

	High-Context	Low-Context
	context of message/action (what is happening around message) carries more meaning than message itself	message seen as separate w/meaning in itself; more attention to message than context
Interpersonal Relationships	dependence on shared info. re: event e.g., less legal paperwork e.g., person's word is bond e.g., depend on power of networks > indiv. e.g., loan $ because of family NOT indiv.	rely on legal bonds, not social bonds e.g., contract > important than spoken word
	depend on social, not legal restraints e.g., don't break law because of what people think not fear of punishment	depend on law to control behavior
	strong feeling of respons. for group e.g., in org. if something wrong, top person takes blame	responsibility passed as far down as poss. ("pass the buck")

Personal Space	more physical closeness e.g., stand closer, touch a lot	concept of "personal space" (people feel violated if this space is invaded) e.g., stand farther, touch less
	less respect for privacy	more respect & desire for privacy
	awareness of body language	less aware of body language
Time	polychronic attitude — everything has "own" time ∴ no one standard of time — punctuality not important — clock time not important	monochronic attitude — everything follows same time — punctuality important — see time as commodity ("time is $")
Advantage	provides social security through social bonds & tradition	more indiv. independence allows greater differences & creativity
Disadvantages	change comes slowly rigid structure may bind people	less commitment to system; less human trust

Cultures on the continuum (ex. from Hall)

Low-context ——————————————————— High-context

German-Swiss German Scandinavian U.S. French English Italian Spanish Greek Arab

* All people unaware of assumptions about reality; unconsciously learn about time, space, etc.
* "mind" is really internalized culture
* important to consider this in multicultural education

LECTURE 10 Earthquakes: Can They Be Predicted?

Earthquakes (EQ) — ~ 30,000 + annually (most minor)

~ 75 significant (many in unpopulated areas)

<u>EQ — "the vibration of the Earth produced by the rapid release of energy"</u>

EQ Cause:

— some caused by atomic explosions or volcanic eruption but infrequent

— most caused by slippage along Earth's crust

— releases energy which radiates from source in waves (like stone dropped in pond)

— Plate tectonics theory: large slabs of Earth's crust — in continual slow motion

— tectonic forces deform rock on both sides of fault (break in rock)

— rocks bend and store energy (like bending wooden stick)

— slippage occurs at weakest point spreading along fault

— releases strain (like stick breaking)

— rock returns (like stretched rubber band) to original shape ("elastic rebound") — these vibrations are EQ

EQ Prediction:

— most research in EQ affected countries

e.g., Japan, U.S., China, Russia

2 types of EQ Prediction Research

Short-Range Prediction

— based on phenomena preceding EQ
  — changes in animal behavior
  — changes in seismic activity
    e.g., quiet followed by
    lot of activity
  — changes in ground water levels
    near faults
  — changes in electric currents or
    radio waves
  — emission of gas (e.g., radon)

Long-Range Prediction

— based on premise that EQs are
  repetitive/cyclical
— scientists look for patterns
  e.g., CA: seismologists said EQ
  occur every 22 yrs... next
  in 1988 but still waiting!
— so far not useful

1 success: China 1975 — evacuated
3 mil. people before major EQ
but scientists skeptical (this area
never had EQs, and suddenly had
tremors) maybe just good guess
(1 yr. later — major EQ not predicted)

Almost all seismologists agree — short-term EQ prediction difficult, if not impossible
Some have hope for long-term prediction

Notes

Notes

Notes

Notes

Notes